DEFINE CAPITAL WITHIN YOUR BUSINESS

MARTIN VAN HELDEN

Define Capital within Your Business

ISBN: 978-1-923512-11-5 (Paperback)

A catalogue record for this book is available from the National Library of Australia.

CLARK & MACKAY

DEAR READER,

Congratulations on your purchase and many thanks from me Author Martin van Helden and my team.

I have created all these business/self-help series to help people get more and deeper understanding of the financial and business world.

Everything in this book is based on existing systems but cannot be taken as financial advice my books are written in the context of helping people to get new insights or ideas or creating new ideas out of this book and use bits as a building block system to create a new idea that works for you.

Reading can be very relaxing and can help you find new ideas and you can take your book wherever you go at any time of the day.

I hope you will enjoy this book and be inspired to read my other books too.

With the highest respect,
Martin van Helden.
Author

CONTENTS

Martin van Helden would like to bring a huge thanks to all the many people who were involved in making this book.

INTRODUCTION

The capital market, with its stocks, bonds, and derivatives, serves as the lifeline of our modern economy. Capital comes in many formats as it can be cash currency (money) or ownership of an asset type or in your employees or hidden deep within your company.

Capital as well as assets is one of the fundamentals of a healthy and very financially strong business, and it gives the organisation a rock-solid base for many years to come.

Capital comes in different forms within your business. It can be financial, human, social, cultural, experiential, intellectual, manufactured, natural, and reputational. They all form a complex web of resources and assets that drive success and growth.

Understanding and if possible, leveraging each type of capital can help businesses address challenges, seize opportunities, and create a sustainable advantage for your business.

This book highlights (top) secrets about capital, and how companies can find the hidden assets with appropriate knowledge of the capital market and compare this with related components of the economy.

It will also highlight (some out of) many things to think about that can help your business grow and create more professional oversite and have a deeper understanding of all the things that mostly are hidden but essential to professionally running a company and how knowledge can be a great help in the forest of rules and procedures of a modern company.

Of course, there is always more to discuss as the corporate world is very large and complex, I made a selection of items to fit the title of this book and hope it will be of great help to you.

As always, I like to emphasize that you can always use your own ideas trough the building block system (in the back of this book) you also need to know that some theories are fixed as they are and do not resonate to this building block system.

As an accountant and a business owner myself, I felt that I needed to help other businesses grow and establish a strong financial base, by sharing the knowledge I have acquired over time regarding capital, asset, and the capital market. There are several other related issues captured in this book, including…

In my countless hours of study and reading books and testing theories myself to seek what can work or not,

I found that intellectual capital is one of the hidden gems within a business. It comprises intangible assets like patents, trademarks, and proprietary knowledge. It is the driving force behind innovation and differentiation. It gives companies a competitive edge in the marketplace. By leveraging intellectual capital, businesses can create unique products, services, and solutions that resonate with customers and set them apart from competitors. This type of capital, unfortunately, in some cases is not given adequate attention by many banks / investors or even business owners today.

For some understanding of the Capital market and the very existence of it we can go back as far as 1602 when the Dutch east indie company (the first company to do so in the world) issued shares that were made tradable on the Amsterdam Stock Exchange.

Transferable shares aim to achieve positive returns on equity, which is evidenced by investment in companies like the Dutch East India Company, which used the financing model to manage their trade on the Indonesian subcontinent.

The Dutch also had established the first Central Bank in 1609 *Amsterdamsche Wisselbank, they defended the coinage standard based on a stable silver bank currency system.*

Even before the Dutch system in Florance Italy there was the Medici Bank (1397-1494) run by the Medici family mostly referred to as "the house of Medici" they were among the first to use the general ledger system of accounting and trough the development of the now widely used Double-entry bookkeeping system (Debit/Credit). This system has the purpose to allow the detection of financial errors and fraud.

To define Capital in your business you may ask Why is this all so important? As you get deeper into defining capital it is an essential to have deep knowledge of most of the ways capital presents itself in your business and in the financial world around you.

When making important financial decisions (for example) that's is one of these moments' knowledge is one of your best friends.

The United. Kingdom. Is the highest net exporter of financial services and London, with its convenient time zone, use of English and feather-light regulations, is one of the world's financial capitals. Lots of cities, including Venice and Amsterdam, have held, and lost the title throughout history.

In the world today it's not the easiest time to run a business / hedge fund / Bank or other financial institute, or work in the financial sector regulations and legal aspects can be very scary and stressful as well.

To keep up to date it is wise to stick to the *NEVER STOP LEARNING* principle like lawyers/doctors/accountants/pilots and some other professionals do and this way keep (deep) knowledge of their profession updated.

This book is a must-have for any (smart) people who are interested in the world of financials and/or are learning to become financially independent.

CHAPTER ONE

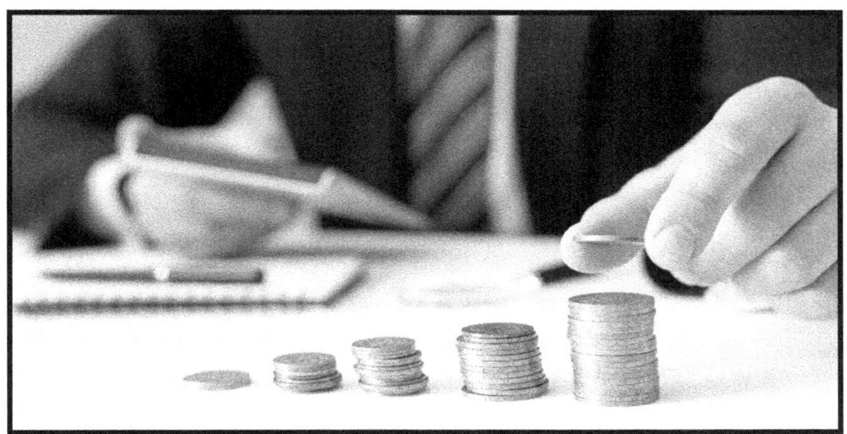

THE FUNCTION OF CURRENCY'S (OR MONEY)

If the function of money is viewed from a wrong angle (like the most working class and middle class get from their childhood), you know the sayings like "Money is the root of evil" "money doesn't make you happy" and more.

The problem starts here, if you have this kind of vision, you cannot have the respect towards money that you need to have to understand the function of money.

Just think about this.... money must have a function as it is in between all kind of transactions.

So, if you look at it without money (cash or electronic) how will transactions be made? Currency (Money) keeps the world on the move.

You know the saying "it's just pieces of paper with pictures on it so we don't need to kill each other when we need something to eat".

Money can also be viewed as a "commodity" as that's what its function basically is, commodities have a market and it's like the stock market it needs to be transacted to live up to its function. (Adam Smith – The Wealth of Nations 1776)

When you view Commodities in the corporate (business) world it has two inputs capital and labour and the price for these are for capital it is interest and for labour it is the labour market (the price people are willing to work for).

Throughout history, commodities and therefore currencies have been known to be instrumental in shaping economic systems and facilitating trade and transactions.

The evolution of currency itself traces back to ancient times when barter systems were prevalent, and people exchanged goods and services directly. As societies grew more complex and trade expanded across regions, the need for a standardized medium of exchange became evident.

The transition from barter to currency marked a notable achievement in the development of economic systems. Various forms of currencies (money)emerged. There were shells then metal coins, and eventually also paper money and now cryptocurrency and algorithm systems to run and calculate the best financial outcome.

STORE OF VALUE

Store of value is an asset, currency, or commodity that maintains its value over a long period. The item would be considered a store of value if its value is either stable or increases over time and doesn't depreciate.

As a store of value, currencies help individuals and businesses to save and hold wealth over longer periods of time. It provides a convenient and widely accepted medium for purchasing all kinds of things. This makes it also possible for people to defer consumption to a later date.

UNIT OF ACCOUNT

As a unit of account, currency provides a standard measure for pricing and valuation. Through the use of a common currency, market participants are able to easily compare prices, track economic performance, and make decisions regarding production and consumption.

In essence, the functions of currency are intertwined with the intricate web of trade and exchange. It shapes the dynamics of global markets and helps to influence economic interactions on a fundamental level.

THE CONCEPT "INVISIBLE HAND"

"Invisible Hand" in economics, introduced by renowned economist Adam Smith in his seminal work "The Wealth of Nations," (1776) is an idea that lays the foundation of economic theory and practice to this day. It posits that individuals pursuing their own self-interest in a free market economy unintentionally benefit society as a whole. This idea suggests that through the interplay of supply and demand, prices, competition, and self-interested actions of individuals, a self-regulating mechanism emerges that guides resources to their most efficient and beneficial uses.

The Invisible Hand metaphorically represents the unseen forces at work in the market that coordinate the actions of individuals and ensure the optimal allocation of resources without the need for centralized planning or control. This helps us gain insights into how markets function, the benefits of competition, and the importance of individual freedom in driving economic prosperity.

HOW DOES THIS CONCEPT INFLUENCE CURRENCY, ECONOMIC STABILITY AND GROWTH?

The value of a currency can fluctuates based on various factors such as supply and demand, geopolitical events, economic indicators, and government policies. In times of economic instability, a country's currency may depreciate rapidly, and that triggers inflation and reduced purchasing power for its citizens. On the other hand, a strong and stable currency can attract foreign investments, promote export growth, and enhance economic prosperity.

Currency exchange rates influence international trade and investment flows, affecting the competitiveness of businesses in global markets. This is why policymakers and businesses try to understand the intricacies of the currency dynamics of the modern economy.

THE ROLE OF CENTRAL BANKS IN THE CURRENCY MARKET

The issuance and regulation of currency became a prerogative of states and governing authorities, and eventually led to the establishment of central banks and monetary systems. The manipulation of currency supply and interest rates became powerful tools in steering economic growth and managing inflation.

These central banks manage currency supply and value, exerting great influence on a nation's economy. They are tasked with the responsibility of regulating the money supply to ensure price stability and promote economic growth in individual nations.

Through mechanisms such as open market operations, reserve requirements, and interest rate adjustments, central banks influence the value of a country's currency in relation to other currencies.

The decisions made by central banks have far-reaching consequences, which affect inflation rates, interest rates, and overall economic stability. Central banks often intervene in currency markets to stabilize exchange rates and prevent excessive fluctuations that could harm the economy. This intervention involves buying or selling currencies to influence their value relative to other currencies, a practice known as foreign exchange intervention.

DIGITAL CURRENCIES AND THEIR IMPACT ON TRADITIONAL CURRENCY SYSTEMS

The rationale behind digital currency goes beyond being a medium of exchange; it embodies a philosophy of decentralization, transparency, and empowerment.

Blockchain technology, the underlying technology behind most digital currencies, ensures trust and immutability in transactions, eliminating the need for intermediaries like banks and financial institutions.

The impact of these currencies on traditional currency systems is profound. Central banks and governments are now grappling with the implications of a decentralized financial system that operates beyond their control. While some see digital currencies as a threat to financial stability and regulation, others view them as a catalyst for innovation and financial inclusion.

As digital currencies continue to evolve and gain mainstream acceptance, it will be fascinating to witness how they reshape the global financial terrain and challenge the very foundations of traditional currency systems. Bitcoin, Ethereum, and other cryptos (as they are fondly called), have gained huge traction because they provide decentralized and (secure) alternatives to traditional government-issued currencies.

The future is undoubtedly being reshaped by the invisible hand of digital currencies.

THE RELATIONSHIP THAT EXISTS BETWEEN INFLATION AND CURRENCY

Inflation refers to the general increase in prices of goods and services over time, resulting in the purchasing power of currency decreasing. This phenomenon is influenced by various factors, including the supply of money in circulation, consumer demand, production costs, and government policies.

Currency influences inflation since it serves as a medium of exchange, store of value, and unit of account. It remains the indispensable cornerstone of the global economy, serving as the lifeline that fuels international trade, investment, and economic growth. The intricate web of currencies, exchange rates, and financial systems intertwine to create a complex yet interconnected network that shapes the economy of the world.

When central banks increase the money supply by printing more currency or implementing expansionary monetary policies, it can lead to inflation as the increased money supply chases the same amount of goods and services, driving up prices. Conversely, when the money supply remains stable or decreases relative to economic output, it can help control inflation or even bring about deflation - a situation where prices decrease over time. Maintaining a balance between the supply of currency and the economic output is essential in controlling inflation and ensuring price stability.

The value of currency relative to other currencies and commodities also influences inflation. Fluctuations in exchange rates and the prices of essential commodities like oil and food can impact on the purchasing power of a currency, which cause inflationary pressures.

HOW DO YOU VIEW CURRENCY (OR MONEY)

There are a lot of ways to look at money but thinking in a practical way and keeping an open mind toward it is very important.

Having emotional barriers toward the financial system or money in particular will not help you to keep an open mind or separate good advice from bad advice, now you need to be indifferent to money but still be in touch with it.

If you have (create) a deep understanding of the function of currency's (money) and have respect for it at the same time, you become indifferent without losing touch with currencies and their market.

Why be indifferent? Well, this also has a function as the amount of money, or transactions raise to mind blowing amounts you will be protected for "greed" of course this is not a guarantee but at least there is a barrier. There is a big difference between “Good” greed and “Bad” greed.

Good greed will stimulate you to take action and provide good opportunities for you and your family as bad greed will harm others and make you blind to all risks.

Having a negative thought against money and saying things like” I can’t afford this” “Money is the root of evil” “money doesn’t make you happy” and more, doesn’t help at all and there not even trough, and it blocks your brain and prevents you from taking the (Richt) action to get you and the organisation to where it needs to be.

Having a positive attitude means you have more impulses, and you can see more opportunities, instead of saying” I can’t afford this” you can say **“What do I need to do to get this done”** and that is a big difference.

It is common for people to have preconceived ideas toward money, and these misconceptions can prevent them from achieving their financial goals. Like I said before, some people are of the opinion that you have to be born into a wealthy family in order to become financially successful. They believe that if they were not born with a silver spoon in their mouth, they would never be able to become wealthy. This belief is simply not true and devastating for you to have a positive thought toward Money and wealth.

There are countless examples of self-made millionaires and billionaires who came from humble beginnings and built their wealth through hard work, determination, and smart financial decisions. Anyone can become one if you follow the financial principles and are disciplined.

Some people are convinced they must have an ultra-high salary to become rich, this is also not true! One doesn't need an ultra-high-paying job in order to become rich. You need the right education (from mentors who are not compromised with double agendas) and be willing to sacrifice all that is needed to get the job done. Many people with modest incomes have been able to amass substantial wealth by living below their means, saving, investing wisely, and taking calculated risks.

Do know that income is just one piece of the wealth-building system, and there are many other avenues to financial success.

As we always say,

"THERE ARE A MILLION WAYS TO MAKE A BUCK"

STAY FOCUSED

In the modern fast moving financial world today, it is very important to stay focused and keep your knowledge up to date. Like accountants and barristers, they need to be up to date also to be able to do a professional job.

The biggest step in life for a lot of people is to let go of certain believes also known as "narrow minded believes" these believes erode your mind and hold you back in keeping an open mind to other point of views, and thus keeping you from moving forward.

An example for a believe like this can be "to make money you need money" if that where trough than everyone who starts a business or owns one was a rich man when they started but we all know about the stories of big entrepreneurs who started with **"zero"** like Richard Brandson , Steve Jobs , Ray Crock (Mc Donalds) , Howard Schultz (Starbucks) or Grand Cardone (Cardone Capital) and many more.

Strive for a healthy work-life balance in pursuit of financial goals. Building wealth takes time, effort, and discipline.

Overnight success stories are few and far between, you know the saying:

"AN OVERNIGHT SUCCESS TAKES 20 YEARS"

Most wealthy individuals have spent years or even decades building their wealth through consistent effort and smart financial decisions. So, make sure you have realistic expectations, and understand that wealth-building is a marathon, not a sprint. Hard work, perseverance, and a willingness to learn and grow are essential components of a successful money-making system, if you hold on to the belief that only a select few have what it takes to become wealthy but instead of this you focus on developing the skills and habits necessary for financial success you will create a more open mind toward these money–making systems, and therefor get a better overview.

LEARN FROM EXPERIENCE

Learn from your experience and I am not only talking about "Financial" experiences but also circumstances that can be bent to clarify the now and then.

Even if you have had situations within your own personal life and every day you collect data and experiences, imagine that you need to find a solution to a problem.

By connecting certain data or experiences you may create the solution you were looking for.

ON TOP OF INFORMATION

Constantly educate yourself about the financial world and follow the changes in the market. Many businesses that have failed in the past did so because they did not adapt to changing economic conditions or did not keep up with industry trends. (like KODAK)

INVOLVE INDUSTRY EXPERTS

Another important lesson we can learn is the value of seeking advice from financial experts. Business failures may occur because management did not seek help when they needed it. For a business to stand firm, it should consult with financial advisors and experts who can give valuable insights and guidance that can help its management make better decisions and avoid costly mistakes.

CREATE REALISTIC GOALS

A business should be realistic about financial goals and expectations. Many businesses that have failed in the past did so because they set unrealistic goals or were overly optimistic about their prospects. Being honest with yourself about your financial situation is important in achieving business goals. Evaluate your financial strengths, business connections, and environment, before setting goals. Simply setting business goals does not make them achievable; it is setting realistic goals that make the difference.

HAVE A LONG-TERM PERSPECTIVE ON FINANCIAL MANAGEMENT

Some businesses that have failed in the past focused too much on short-term gains and did not consider the long-term implications of their financial decisions. Set yourself up for financial success by only taking a long-term view and planning for the future.

Learning from past business failures helps you gain valuable insights that can help you handle money better. Research the mistakes that others have made and take steps to avoid making the same errors. It is important to budget, save, avoid debt, diversify income streams, stay informed, seek advice, set realistic goals, and take a long-term perspective when it comes to handling money.

MAKE A NEW/FLEXIBLE PLAN AND ADJUST AS YOU MOVE ON.

To make a big change to your business is not without risks and resistance, so to be able to cope with the changing environment it can be verry helpful to have a flexible plan with multiple site ways that always lead to the same outcome for your success.

Also, very important to keep in mind that your plans/approach to all solutions needs to be “flexible” so you can adjust your plans when needed, for example you make a plan but 2 years later the environment around you change rapidly and it no longer works so you need to be able to “adjust” the plan to the new needs.

This way you don’t need to rethink everything only the components that need to be adjusted and that saves you time and Struggles or Stress.

(Read my first book “turning daily struggle into opportunities” ISBN978-1-6698-3391-8)

Create a reward system to make sure there is something to look forward to when completing the task, it doesn’t need to be money it can also mean a company car a day to the beach or a museum day or (if it is entirely for yourself) buying stuff for your hobby go and take a ride or even take a holyday to an exotic place.

This will stimulate the brain to be more active and when achieving this it will give you an even bigger boost to go ahead with your projects.

In my book" How passion can make a business" (ISBN978-1-922784-79-7) I explain "How to setup effective reward systems".

A flexible business plan is a dynamic document that can be easily adjusted to meet the needs of a company as its environment changes. My saying would be if you don't handle "currency" with care, it may not last for long. Companies must create a system to be able to adapt to the ever-changing environments to ensure their businesses are not affected significantly, at any given time. This is where creating that very important (flexible) business plan comes into play.

To create a flexible business plan, you need to do market research tailormade to your company. Analyze current trends in the industry, as well as potential changes that may occur in the near future. It provides you with information about the external environment and ever-changing consumers. That helps a business to better anticipate and prepare for any disruptions that may affect your business in the future.

Involve your employees in the planning process. Their input will help you tap into a pool of knowledge and expertise that will help your business plan. It will also increase buy-in and commitment from them.

Be willing to do trials and experiments before introducing them to the market and take calculated risks. By testing new ideas and strategies, you can learn what works and what doesn't, and adjust your business plans accordingly. This willingness to innovate and take risks can help your business stay competitive as well.

What steps can a business take to make their business plans more flexible and responsive to changing environments?

Review and Update Plans: Business plans are the roadmaps that guide businesses toward their goals and objectives.

Reviewing and updating them will ensure that an organization is on track to achieve its desired goals. Not only that, but it also means that it can make necessary adjustments to address any changes in its environment or production process. This is because the business environment constantly evolves. New technologies, global trends, and competitive forces can all impact the business's operations and strategy. This is why organizations need to update their plans, to stay ahead of these changes and adapt their strategies to remain competitive.

You review your business plan to identify any weaknesses or inefficiencies in current strategies. It is always helpful to check your performance (KPI's) against your original goals and objectives. This will help you pinpoint areas where you may be falling short so you can make adjustments. Your organization will be able to stay focused on its long-term vision. It's easy for businesses to get caught up in day-to-day operations and lose sight of their overarching goals. Revisiting business plans on a regular basis can ensure that they are staying true to their mission and making decisions that are in line with their strategic objectives.

So, when you update your business plans, you will find it easy to communicate your goals and priorities to stakeholders.

This also helps to build trust and confidence in the organization's leadership and heading of the company. It reveals that they are proactive and responsive to changes in the market.

Business plans are also reviewed to ensure that resources are being allocated effectively. A good management team must know where to invest their time, money, and manpower. This can help to maximize efficiency and drive better performance.

If the business treat their business plans as (living) documents that require constant monitoring and adjustments to ensure that they continue to serve as effective roadmaps for achieving success it will be much more embedded within the organization structure. Conducting regular reviews of their plans can help them identify potential threats and develop contingency plans to mitigate them.

Utilize Scenario Planning: Scenario planning is a strategic management tool used by businesses to anticipate and plan for different future occurrences that may impact the organization.

This approach can help businesses to be more flexible and adaptable in their decision-making process.

Traditional business plans are often rigid and do not account for changes in the market or unexpected events that may impact the organization. In contrast, a flexible business plan allows businesses to adapt to changing circumstances and make strategic decisions based on the best available information.

Scenario planning makes businesses think strategically about the future and consider a wide range of factors that may impact the organization. They analyze trends, market dynamics, competitive pressures, regulatory changes, and other external factors that may influence the business environment. It encourages businesses to be more open-minded and innovative in their decision-making process.

Make Your Decision-Making Agile: The agile decision-making processes can help your company to quickly respond to changing market conditions, customer demands, and other external factors that may impact on its operations. This can be especially important in industries that are highly competitive or subject to rapid technological advancements. Such companies can stay ahead of the curve and take advantage of new opportunities as they arise. This flexibility also allows businesses to better manage risks and uncertainties, reducing the likelihood of costly mistakes or missed opportunities.

Your ability to quickly identify and address problems before they escalate is very important in business. Companies regularly monitor key performance indicators (KPI's) and make data-driven decisions, so that they can proactively address issues and mitigate risks without being caught off guard.

You can foster a sense of accountability and teamwork among your employees by simply empowering them to make decisions and take ownership of their work. This can lead to increased productivity, higher job satisfaction, and enhanced work performance.

Monitor Key Performance Indicators (KPIs): Identify key metrics that indicate the health of your business and track them regularly. Use this data to make informed decisions about where adjustments may be needed in your plan.

Key performance indicators (KPI's) are important metrics that help businesses measure their performance against their goals and objectives. It means you need to set clear and specific goals for your business. These goals should be realistic, measurable, and aligned with the company's mission and values. When you do this, you will be able to better track your progress and performance against your business objectives.

That being said, for your specific business you need to identify and establish what the right metrics will be to track. Not all KPIs are created equal, so it's important to identify the most relevant metrics for your business. This could include financial metrics such as revenue growth and

profitability, operational metrics such as customer satisfaction and employee productivity. Marketing metrics such as conversion rates and customer acquisition costs.

Once you have identified the key metrics to track, monitor, and analyze these KPIs. You can create dashboards or reports to track progress, conduct regular meetings to review performance and identify trends or patterns that may require action. It helps you spot potential issues or problems early on and take corrective action. It will easily uncover areas of improvement, make adjustments to your business strategies or processes, and ultimately enhance their performance.

This practice is also good if you want to benchmark yourself against competitors or industry standards. You can compare your performance against others in the industry, identify areas where they may be falling behind, and take steps to improve and stay competitive.

By monitoring KPIs you can provide yourself with valuable insights into customer behavior, market trends, and industry dynamics and therefore creating a stronger base for the company and its future.

Ensure Collaboration Across Departments: Gone are the days when departments could independently function without the need to communicate and align their efforts. Organizations foster a culture of collaboration and teamwork among their various teams. They must ensure that different departments work together seamlessly towards the common goal of the organization. This not only improves communication within the company but also increases efficiency and productivity. When employees from different departments collaborate on projects, they bring together diverse perspectives and skill sets that entertain innovative solutions and better business outcomes.

Collaboration across departments helps to break down barriers and create a more cohesive work environment. When employees feel that they are part of a larger team working towards a common goal, they are more motivated and engaged in their work. This sense of unity can result in higher employee morale and lower turnover rates.

But this requires strong leadership and communication skills. Leaders need to set the tone for collaboration by encouraging open communication, fostering teamwork, and creating a sense of trust among employees. They need to provide the necessary resources and support to help teams work together effectively.

In addition to leadership support, companies can provide tools and technologies to facilitate collaboration among departments. In **Japan** they developed a set of policies and procedures called **"KAIZEN"** it is developed to improve all stages of production and overall quality as well as the collaboration and communication between all staff.

Project management software, communication platforms, and collaboration tools can also help teams share information, track progress, and work together more efficiently. These tools can also help to break down silos and promote cross-departmental collaboration.

Build Strong Relationships with Suppliers and Partners: If you want long-term success for your business, you must build strong relationships with your suppliers and business partners. These relationships can provide useful insights into market trends, potential risks, and opportunities for growth. How Can this be achieved?

Communication: It is important to establish open lines of communication from the very beginning of the relationship. This communication should be two-way, with both parties actively listening to each other›s needs and concerns. Regular meetings and check-ins can help ensure that both parties are on the same page and can address any issues that may arise quickly and effectively.

Trust: Trust is the foundation of any successful relationship, and it is important to demonstrate trustworthiness and reliability in all of your interactions. Do well to deliver on all your promises, be transparent about your business practices, and treat your partners with respect and be professional.

See Them as Partners: It is better to view your relationship with suppliers and business partners as a partnership, rather than a transactional relationship. This means working together to achieve common goals and finding ways to create mutual value. Make sure you work with only suppliers and partners whose interests align with yours. All will be able to work towards a shared vision and create a strong foundation for a successful and long-lasting partnership/collaborations.

Appreciation: Recognizing their contributions and showing gratitude for their hard work and dedication can go a long way in strengthening your relationship with people/employees. You can do this through simple gestures such as thank-you notes or small gifts, as well as through larger initiatives such as joint marketing campaigns or collaborations.

INVEST IN EMPLOYEE TRAINING

Equipping your team with the right skills they need to thrive in a changing environment is never a loss.

Organizations are constantly looking for ways to stay ahead of the curve. One strategy that has been proven to be effective in achieving this goal is investing in employee training. They provide ongoing learning opportunities for their team members. It develops them and also empowers them to adapt to changing environments. And when employees are equipped with the right skills and knowledge, they are more able to perform their roles effectively and efficiently. Such a strategy leads to increased output, higher quality work, and ultimately, greater profitability for the business.

One thing many business owners don't know is that providing ongoing training opportunities to your employees can help future-proof your business. As technologies and industries continue to evolve, employees need to stay updated on the latest trends and developments in their field. So, when you invest in training programs, you are ensuring that your team is equipped to adapt to changing circumstances and remain competitive in the marketplace. Think about it. It's a plus to your business, however you view it.

HAVE A STRONG WORKING CAPITAL AND ASSET BASE

Every business needs financial stability and flexibility to weather any storms that may come its way.

Having a strong working capital ensures that your business can continue to operate smoothly even during times when clients may not be paying their bills on time. This is especially important for small businesses that may have limited cash reserves. You can keep your business running and pay your bills on time, thereby maintaining a good reputation with suppliers and creditors.

A strong working capital will enable your business to take advantage of opportunities for growth and expansion, including investing in new equipment, launching a new product line, or expanding into new markets. Having the necessary funds readily available can help your business seize these opportunities without having to rely on external financing.

Building a strong asset base for your company is equally important. Assets such as equipment, inventory, and property can provide stability and value to your business. They can also be used as collateral for securing loans or financing.

Below I have summed up nine (9) strategies businesses can use to build a strong working capital and asset base.

Effective Cash Flow Management: Cash flow management involves monitoring and controlling the flow of cash in and out of your company in order to ensure that you have enough liquid assets to cover your operational expenses. Without effective cash flow management, businesses can run into financial difficulties and even face the risk of insolvency.

A good business has to monitor cash flow on a regular basis. This involves tracking both your incoming cash from sales and other sources, as well as your outgoing cash for expenses such as rent, payroll, and supplies. It also involves careful budgeting for your operational costs and finding ways to reduce unnecessary spending. Management should cut costs where possible, to free up cash that can be used to cover expenses during lean times or reinvested back into business to promote growth.

In addition to monitoring and controlling your cash flow, have a plan in place for managing cash shortages. Try to secure a line of credit or a business loan to cover short-term cash needs or negotiate extended payment terms with suppliers to improve cash flow. Effective cash flow management requires careful planning and attention to detail.

Maintain Optimal Inventory Levels: Ensuring that you have the right amount of stock on hand can help prevent stockouts, reduce excess inventory holding costs, and improve efficiency and profitability.

Safety stock is the extra inventory kept on hand to account for unexpected increases in demand or delays in the supply chain. Your business needs to have this at all times. Why? Having it helps you reduce the risk of stockouts and ensure that you can fulfill customer orders in a timely manner.

One key factor in maintaining optimal inventory levels is keeping track of your inventory turnover rate. This refers to the number of times your inventory is sold and replaced over a specific period of time. It will help you identify trends in demand and adjust your ordering quantities accordingly to prevent stock shortages or overstock situations. You should also review and adjust your reorder points and order quantities based on demand forecasts and lead times. Optimize your order quantities and schedules so that you can minimize carrying costs while ensuring that you always have enough stock on hand to meet customer demand.

Implementing a reliable inventory management system helps streamline your inventory control processes and provides real-time insights into your stock levels and performance. You can do this by leveraging technology to automate inventory tracking. That will help you reduce manual errors, improve accuracy, and make data-driven decisions to maintain optimal inventory levels.

Manage Accounts Receivable: Accounts receivable refer to the outstanding payments that the business is owed by its customers for goods or services rendered. Managing accounts receivable helps to maintain a healthy financial position for any business. Efficiently managing accounts receivable can help a business improve cash flow and maintain a positive relationship with customers.

Ensure you implement efficient invoicing and collection processes to shorten the accounts receivable cycle and improve cash flow. Send out invoices promptly after the goods or services have been delivered, clearly stating the payment terms and due date, and providing multiple payment options for customers. You will both make it easy for customers to pay, reduce the time it takes to receive payment and improve your cash flow.

One other way to manage accounts receivable is collection processes. Businesses should have clear policies in place for following up on overdue payments, including sending out reminder notices, making phone calls, and possibly implementing late fees for delinquent accounts. They need to strike a balance between being firm in collecting payments and maintaining a positive relationship with customers.

There are many software solutions available that can automate invoicing processes, track overdue payments, and send out reminders to customers. For example... You can leverage technology to streamline accounts receivable processes and reduce the time and resources spent on manual tasks.

Negotiate Favorable Payment Terms: One way to improve your liquidity and preserve working capital is by negotiating favorable payment terms with your suppliers. By extending the time you have to pay your bills, you can free up cash to invest in other areas of your business or weather any unexpected financial challenges that may arise.

Here are some tips to help you anytime you want to negotiate favorable payment terms for your business:

- **Establish a good relationship with your suppliers:** Building a strong relationship with your suppliers can go a long way in negotiating favorable payment terms. Show them that you are a reliable and trustworthy partner by paying your bills on time and communicating openly about your financial situation.
- **Know your financial position:** Before entering into negotiations with your suppliers, have a clear understanding of your financial position. This includes knowing your current cash flow, profitability, and any upcoming expenses that may impact on your ability to make timely payments.
- **Highlight the benefits to your suppliers:** When negotiating payment terms, be sure to emphasize the benefits to your suppliers of extending the time you have to pay. For example, longer payment terms can lead to increased order sizes,

more consistent business, and improved cash flow for your suppliers.

- **Offer something in return:** To sweeten the deal, consider offering something in return for extended payment terms - maybe early payment discounts, guaranteed volumes of orders, or exclusive rights to your business.
- **Be flexible and willing to compromise:** Negotiating payment terms is a two-way street, so be prepared to listen to your suppliers› concerns and be willing to find a compromise that works for both parties. The goal is to reach an agreement that benefits both your business and your suppliers.

Invest Wisely in Fixed Assets: Fixed assets provide long-term value and a competitive advantage. They range from tangible items such as property and equipment to intangible assets such as patents or trademarks. Tangible fixed assets are (real) physical

items that can be seen, touched, and felt, while intangible fixed assets are non-physical assets that provide long-term value to a business.

Fixed assets provide a source of long-term value and competitive advantage for a business. For instance, investing in new technology can improve production capacity and efficiency, in a shorter amount of time. Fixed assets equally serve as collateral for financing opportunities.

When investing in fixed assets, carefully consider the costs and benefits of acquiring such assets, as a cost-benefit analysis should be conducted to determine whether the investment will provide a return on investment. Other cost-factors to consider include maintenance and repair costs, as well as the potential for obsolescence and technological advancements. Like, investing in new technology may provide short-term benefits, but the technology may quickly become outdated, requiring further investment in the future.

Diversify your Revenue Streams: Relying on a single source of income makes businesses leave themselves vulnerable to market fluctuations and economic downturns. This is why you need to diversify your revenue streams: you need to expand product lines, enter new markets, or offer additional services to reach a broader customer base and generate multiple income streams. (often called omni channeling)

To effectively diversify your revenue streams, start by conducting a comprehensive analysis of your current market position and consumer needs. Look for potential gaps in your product or service offerings that could be monetized. Consider exploring partnerships, licensing agreements, or subscriptions to tap into new revenue sources. You can also leverage market research and customer feedback to identify emerging trends and opportunities for expansion.

However, you need to evaluate each potential opportunity for its feasibility and long-term sustainability. You can achieve this by conducting a thorough analysis of the market demand, competition, and regulatory environment to assess the viability of each new revenue stream. Consider factors such as scalability, resource requirements, and potential risks before committing to any new initiatives. That will ensure a higher likelihood of success and profitability in the long run.

Once you have identified viable revenue stream opportunities (omni channeling), move on to developing a clear implementation plan. Allocate resources efficiently, set measurable objectives, and establish key performance indicators to track progress effectively. Communicate the new revenue stream initiatives within your organization to ensure alignment and support from all stakeholders. Then, monitor market dynamics and customer feedback closely, making necessary adjustments as you go to optimize the performance of each revenue stream.

Regularly review financial metrics and performance indicators to gauge the success of your diversification strategy. The key to having a winning concept or plan is flexibility.

Identify which streams are performing well and allocate resources strategically to scale them further. Use cross-promotion and bundling strategies to enhance customer value and create synergies between different revenue streams. Also, consider reinvesting profits from successful streams into new areas of growth or innovation.

Monitor and Analyze Financial Ratios: Always keep a close eye on key financial ratios like the current ratio, quick ratio, and debt-to-equity ratio to assess the health of your working capital and asset base.

CURRENT RATIO

The current ratio is a key indicator of a company's ability to meet its short-term obligations. It is calculated by dividing current assets by current liabilities. A ratio of 2:1 is generally considered healthy, as it indicates that a company has enough assets to cover its current liabilities. A ratio below 1 may indicate financial trouble, as it suggests that a company may struggle to pay its bills on time.

QUICK RATIO

The quick ratio, also known as the acid-test ratio, measures a company's ability to meet its short-term obligations using its most liquid assets. It excludes inventory from current assets, as inventory may not be easily converted into cash. A quick ratio of 1:1 is generally considered ideal, as it indicates that a company can cover its short-term liabilities without relying on inventory sales.

DEBT-TO-EQUITY RATIO

The debt-to-equity ratio indicates a company's financial leverage. It measures the proportion of debt to equity in a company's capital structure. A high debt-to-equity ratio may indicate that a company is relying too heavily on debt to finance its operations, which can increase financial risk. On the other hand, a low debt-to-equity ratio may indicate that a company is not taking advantage of potential growth opportunities.

Every company can always monitor and analyze these financial ratios, to identify areas of improvement, such as reducing debt levels or increasing liquid assets. If these monitors are done on a regular base this approach can help companies avoid cash flow problems, improve profitability, and achieve long-term success.

Plan for Contingencies: Reserve funds can provide a safety net for your business during uncertain times, as every businessman desires to cover essential expenses and keep operations running smoothly. A reserve fund acts as a financial buffer. It safeguards your business against unforeseen circumstances such as unexpected expenses or economic downturns. Such a financial cushion provides stability and peace of mind, which enables you to deal with challenges with confidence.

How do you go about this?

CREATE A BUDGET AND SET ASIDE FUNDS

Prioritize essential expenses and allocate a percentage of your revenue specifically for the fund. Regularly review and adjust your budget to ensure that your reserve fund remains adequately funded. Setting clear financial goals and tracking your progress can provide insights into your cash flow patterns and help you make informed decisions to protect your business during unforeseen downturns.

INVEST EXCESS CASH WISELY

Once you have built a healthy reserve fund, consider investing any excess cash strategically. Explore low-risk investment options such as money market accounts or short-term bonds to increase your returns while safe-guarding your funds. Diversify your investments to mitigate risks and ensure liquidity when needed. Also, consult with a financial advisor to tailor an investment strategy that aligns with your business goals and risk tolerance.

UTILIZE BUSINESS LINES OF CREDIT OR LOANS AS A BACKUP

Having access to business lines of credit or loans can provide a valuable safety net during times of unexpected expenses or economic downturns.

Establishing relationships with reputable financial institutions can help you secure favorable terms and quick access to additional funds when needed. Be sure to carefully evaluate the terms and conditions of any credit or loans to ensure they align with your business's financial goals.

MONITOR AND ADJUST YOUR RESERVE FUND AS NEEDED

Regularly review your business's cash flow and reassess the adequacy of your reserve fund based on current economic conditions and upcoming expenses. Set aside a percentage of your profits each month to replenish or increase your reserve fund. Stay informed about industry trends and economic indicators that may impact your business's financial health.

Review Financial Performance Regularly: Regularly reviewing financial performance can provide valuable insights into the health of a company's finances, identify areas of improvement, and highlight potential risks.

How do you review your financial performance?

SET THE RIGHT METRICS FOR EVALUATION

Key financial metrics such as liquidity ratios, profitability ratios, and efficiency ratios are necessary in assessing the health of your company's working capital. You can gain a deeper understanding of your financial strengths and weaknesses and make informed decisions to improve your working capital by establishing and monitoring those metrics regularly.

ANALYZE CASH FLOW AND PROFITABILITY

Once you have established the key financial metrics for evaluating your working capital, move on to your cash flow and profitability. Analyzing your cash flow will help you understand how money is moving in and out of your business, highlighting any potential areas of improvement or concern. Similarly, assessing profitability ratios will give you insights into your company's ability to generate profits and sustain growth over time. Scrutinizing both aspects of your financial performance will help you make strategic decisions to strengthen your working capital and drive long-term success.

IDENTIFY TRENDS AND POTENTIAL ISSUES

After analyzing cash flow and profitability, the next step is to identify trends and potential issues within your financial data. Make sure you track patterns over time, to spot emerging issues or opportunities that may impact your working capital. Look for consistent trends in cash flow, profitability, and other key metrics to proactively address any potential challenges. Also, investigate any fluctuations or anomalies that could signify underlying problems that need immediate attention.

MAKE DECISIONS TO IMPROVE YOUR WORKING CAPITAL

Once you have identified trends and potential issues in your financial performance data, it is crucial to make informed decisions to enhance your working capital.

Utilize the insights gained from analyzing cash flow, profitability, and key metrics to develop strategic initiatives that optimize working capital efficiency. Implement measures such as inventory management improvements, tightening credit terms, or negotiating supplier discounts.

To fortify your financial position, consider implementing strategies that align with the insights gleaned from your company's financial performance review. Evaluate opportunities to improve operational efficiency, streamline processes, and diversify revenue streams. Implement cost-saving initiatives and monitor key performance indicators regularly to track progress. Then, explore options to optimize your capital structure and manage the debt levels effectively.

"The love of money," they say, "is the root of all evil." Notice that money itself is not the root of evil but the love. The 'love' here refers to greed. We need money to achieve literally anything we wish to accomplish in business. So, avoiding money or being scared about accumulating a lot of it is unwise.

The golden rule is never be too greedy that you don't carefully calculate the risk of a loss in your attempt to make money. This is the right perspective to money making, especially for potential investors.

CHAPTER TWO

DOUBLE COINCIDENCE OF WANTS (BARTER)

As one of the earliest economic systems, barter was once the main form of obtaining necessary goods and services. It is the foundation of commerce. Barter exchanges helped develop marketplaces for trade and influenced social structures within ancient societies.

The ancient art of trading is an effective tool for getting what you want. However, barter requires a certain level of finesse.

Almost all civilizations of the world at some point in time relied on the barter system, where people exchanged goods and services for other goods and services in return. It is called the ***"double coincidence of wants."*** It has its own advantages; for example, it does not require any additional item (cash) for transactions, it helps people fulfill their needs by exchanging things that they already have, and it is a mutually negotiated deal that does not involve any other party.

This trade system remains a mode of transaction for the masses in societies whenever there is a monetary crisis, like the failure of the centralized banking system leading to money being in short supply or high devaluation because of hyperinflation.

During the Great Depression of the 1930s, barter became a way of transaction for a larger number of people due to the short supply of money, and similarly, as recently as in 2019 people relied on barter because of their currency devaluation during the Venezuelan crisis.

UNDERSTANDING OF DOUBLE COINCIDENCE OF WANTS

In any economy, one of the most fundamental challenges that individuals face is the double coincidence of wants. This economic problem arises when two parties desiring to engage in a trade must each possess a good or service that the other party needs or wants. The double coincidence of wants can create barriers to efficient exchange and necessitates the development of mediums of exchange to overcome this hurdle.

In principle, a double coincidence of wants would mean that both parties must agree to sell and buy each commodity. Under this system, problems can arise through the improbability of the wants, needs, or events that cause or motivate a transaction occurring at the same time and in the same place.

One example is the bar musician who is "paid" with liquor or food, items that his landlord will not accept as rent payment when the musician would rather have a month's shelter. If, instead, the musician's landlord where to throw a party and desire music for it, hiring the musician to play it by offering the month's rent in exchange, a coincidence of wants would exist.

The double coincidence of wants problem arises when two parties are attempting to engage in a barter transaction, but each party only has goods or services that the other party does not want or need. In other words, there is a mismatch of wants between the two parties, making trade difficult.

IMPACT OF MODERN TECHNOLOGY ON BARTER AND TRADE

As trends in technology and sustainability continue to evolve and merge, it becomes apparent that barter has the potential to play an increasingly influential role in future economic and financial systems. The next few decades could very well witness significant strides in this age-old trading system, potentially reshaping the global economy in unique or newly developed ways.

Modern barter and trade have evolved considerably to become an effective method of increasing sales, conserving cash, moving inventory, and making use of excess production capacity for businesses around the world. Businesses in a barter earn trade credits (instead of cash) that are deposited into their account. They then have the ability to purchase goods and services from other members utilizing their trade credits – they are not obligated to purchase from those whom they sold to, and / or vice versa.

The exchange plays an important role because it provides record-keeping, brokering expertise, and monthly statements to each member. Commercial exchanges make money by charging a commission on each transaction - either all on the buy side, all on the sell side, or a combination of both. A successful example are the International Monetary Systems, which was founded in 1985 and is one of the first exchanges in North America opened after the TEFRA Act of 1982.

THE DIFFERENCE BETWEEN ASSETS AND LIABILITIES

Assets are resources that bring value to a business or individual, while liabilities are obligations that require payments or sacrifices. Distinguishing between the two is instrumental in evaluating financial health and making strategic investment choices. To ensure effective cash-flow management, one must optimize asset growth while minimizing liabilities.

CLARITY ON ASSETS

Assets are resources that a business owns or controls, which can be used to generate future economic benefits. In the operations of a business, assets serve as the backbone that allows for smooth functioning and sustainable growth.

They enhance operational efficiency and contribute to the overall success and profitability of a company.

Assets can be grouped into tangible or intangible. Tangible assets are physical items like machinery, equipment, inventory, and real estate that hold inherent value and can be touched or seen. Intangible assets, such as intellectual property, patents, trademarks, and goodwill, lack physical form but are equally valuable for a company's success. Intangible assets like intellectual property and goodwill can be leveraged to enhance brand reputation, attract investors, and create long-term value.

DEALING WITH LIABILITIES

Every business owner needs to understand and manage liability properly. Business liability encompasses a wide range of legal obligations that a company must comply with to avoid financial risks and legal repercussions. It can include debts, contractual obligations, and responsibilities towards employees, customers, and other stakeholders.

Properly managing it involves assessing and mitigating potential risks, such as lawsuits, financial losses, or breaches of contracts. Proactively addressing liabilities also enhances your credibility with stakeholders and reinforces trust in your business practices.

NEED FOR LIABILITY INSURANCE

A business owner should have liability insurance to protect their business. Liability insurance has various forms, each tailored to address specific risks faced by businesses. General liability insurance covers costs related to third-party bodily injuries or property damage on your business premises. Whereas, professional liability insurance, also known as errors and omissions insurance, safeguards against claims of negligence or inadequate services.

There is also product liability insurance, which protects against liabilities arising from defects in products you manufacture or sell. Then, there is cyber liability insurance that shields your business from financial losses due to data breaches or cyberattacks.

Operating without adequate business liability insurance can expose your business to legal risks. In the event of a lawsuit or claim against your company, not having proper coverage could result in hefty out-of-pocket expenses and financial ruin. Without insurance, you may be personally liable for damages, settlements, legal fees, and other costs associated with a lawsuit.

Determining the appropriate amount of coverage for your business liability insurance is vital for adequate protection. Factors such as your industry, business size, and the level of risk involved should be considered when evaluating coverage needs. Your management team needs to conduct a thorough risk assessment to identify potential liabilities and assess the financial impact of worst-case scenarios. It is advised that they work with insurance professionals to understand policy terms and coverage limits.

Keep in mind that underinsuring can leave your business vulnerable, while over insuring may lead to unnecessary costs. Having the right balance ensures your business is well-protected without overspending on premiums. Then, you have to review and adjust your coverage as your business grows and risks evolve.

To calculate if your business is adequately protected, follow these 5 steps:

1. Assess your business›s specific liability risks and needs.
2. Consult with insurance professionals to explore suitable coverage options.
3. Compare quotes and coverage details from different insurers.
4. Review your policy annually and adjust coverage as your business grows.
5. Stay informed about changes in regulations and industry standards that may impact your coverage needs.

INVESTING IN ASSETS TO IMPROVE CASH FLOW

A business that invests in assets can improve their cash flow and increase their efficiency and productivity. Initiatives like technology upgrades and real estate acquisitions are ways to invest in business assets. In investing in assets, don't choose those that only generate immediate returns. Rather opt for assets with the potential for sustained growth. Diversifying asset portfolios, leveraging technology for efficiency gains, and aligning investments with market trends are effective strategies to consider.

Once you have implemented asset investments, continuously monitor and adjust your investment strategies. Ensure that you always review financial performance and market trends. Doing that will help you to identify areas for improvement and make necessary adjustments to optimize your asset investments.

HOW DO YOU MAINTAIN A HEALTHY FINANCIAL BALANCE?

Maintaining a healthy financial balance protects against unexpected emergencies and enables individuals and businesses to seize opportunities for growth. A balanced mix of assets and liabilities helps in diversifying risk and ensuring financial security in the long run. When one consistently monitors and manages their assets and liabilities, they can adapt to changing economic conditions and align their financial goals accordingly.

To ensure a healthy financial balance, you need to implement strategies that optimize your assets. You can do this by conducting a detailed assessment of your current assets and considering diversification to spread risk. Try to explore investment opportunities that align with your financial goals and risk tolerance. Regularly review and adjust your asset allocation to adapt to market fluctuations. Also, focus on building an emergency fund to protect against unforeseen expenses.

Assets such as real estate, stocks, and business investments hold the potential to generate income and increase in value over time. Leverage these assets by making informed decisions, conducting regular assessments, and adapting to market fluctuations. With a proactive approach to asset management, you can secure a stable financial foundation and pave the way for sustained prosperity.

DIFFERENT TYPES OF DEBT

Debt is a common aspect of running a business, as it often provides the necessary funds for growth and expansion. However, not all debt is created equal, and different types of debt can have varying impacts on your company's ability to repay. Knowing these differences helps a business make informed financial decisions.

Understanding the purpose and repayment timeline of each type of debt is key to maintaining a healthy financial position and ensuring your company's long-term sustainability.

COMPARING DEBTS

(Short-Term Debt vs Long-Term Debt)

SHORT-TERM DEBT

Short-term debt is a common financial instrument used by businesses to meet immediate cash flow needs. Unlike long-term debt, which is typically repaid over several years, short-term debt must be repaid within a year. This type of debt can take many forms, including credit lines, accounts payable, and short-term loans. Short-term debt helps to maintain a company's liquidity and fund immediate operational needs.

Short-term debt comes in various forms, each serving different purposes and carrying unique characteristics. Common types include trade credit, lines of credit, commercial paper, and short-term loans. Understanding the distinctions between these types is essential for businesses to assess which options align best with their financial objectives and cash flow requirements.

When utilizing short-term debt for financing needs, businesses must carefully weigh the risks and benefits associated with each type. While short-term debt can provide quick access to funds and help manage cash flow fluctuations, it also comes with risks such as higher interest rates and potential liquidity issues.

Effectively managing short-term debt requires a strategic approach to balance financial needs and risks. One essential strategy is to carefully assess your business's cash flow projections and financing requirements to determine the appropriate amount of short-term debt to take on. You can also monitor interest rates and repayment schedules to avoid unnecessary costs and liquidity challenges. Utilizing short-term debt for revenue-generating activities, such as inventory restocking or equipment upgrades, can optimize its benefits while minimizing risks.

LONG-TERM DEBT

Long-term debt can vary based on the financial needs and goals of a business. Common types of it include bonds, mortgages, and long-term loans.

Bonds involve borrowing money from investors and paying interest over a specific period. Mortgages are loans secured by real estate assets, often used for property purchases.

Long-term loans are borrowed funds repaid over an extended period, typically with a fixed interest rate. With long-term debt, you can access larger amounts of capital compared to short-term financing options. This can facilitate strategic investments, expansions, and acquisitions that would not be feasible with limited funding sources. Long-term debt often comes with lower interest rates. They offer cost savings over the loan term. Moreover, fixed repayment schedules offer predictability and stability to cash flow management, assisting in long-term financial planning.

It is imperative for businesses to also consider the potential drawbacks associated with this form of financing. For example, the long-term commitment and obligation to repay the borrowed amount over an extended period can limit financial flexibility and strain cash flow in the long run. Again, businesses may face challenges if unable to meet repayment obligations, leading to financial distress or credit rating implications. The cumulative cost of borrowing over time due to accruing interest payments can also impact profitability and financial performance.

SECURED DEBT VS UNSECURED DEBT

Secured debt involves collateral, providing a safety net for lenders in case of default, while unsecured debt relies solely on creditworthiness.

SECURED DEBT

Secured debt is commonly used for significant purchases that require long-term financing, such as buying a building, vehicle, production machinery or financing a takeover. If a borrower offers collateral, such as the property itself or the vehicle being purchased, they can secure lower interest rates and more extended repayment terms. Mortgages are a prime example of secured debt that enables businesses to fulfill their goals and spreading out payments over decades.

SECURED DEBT IN PRACTICE:

The use of secured debt can be seen when the business leverages their assets or vehicles / machinery to secure financing for goals to be achieved.

Similarly for the consumer, obtaining a vehicle through a car loan facilitates transportation for work and daily activities, which enhances quality of life. Secured debt enables individuals to make large purchases that may not be feasible with immediate cash on hand.

MANAGING SECURED DEBT:

Managing secured debt is inevitable if you look to maintain financial stability and ensure the protection of your assets. Effective management of secured debt requires diligence and a proactive approach to financial planning.

Here are some key points to consider when managing secured debt:

Make Timely Payments: Ensure that you make your secured debt payments on time to avoid default and loss of collateral. Setting up automatic payments or creating reminders can help you stay on track with your repayment schedule.

Budget Wisely: Developing a budget that prioritizes your secured debt payments can help you allocate funds efficiently. You must understand your financial obligations and income sources. That will drive you to get the necessary funds for your loan repayments.

Plan for the Long Term: Secured debt often comes with longer payment terms, providing you with flexibility in managing your finances. So, you can take advantage of this by creating a repayment plan based on your financial goals.

UNSECURED DEBT

In contrast, unsecured debt serves a different purpose as it provides funding for smaller expenses or consolidates existing debt. Without the need for collateral, unsecured debt relies solely on the borrower's creditworthiness.

Credit cards are a prevalent form of unsecured debt that enables businesses / individuals to make purchases and pay them off over time. Small business loans, Personal loans, student loans, and medical loans are examples of unsecured debt. The flexibility of unsecured debt lies in its ability to offer funds without requiring collateral.

MANAGEMENT OF UNSECURED DEBT:

When it comes to managing unsecured debt, every business needs to stay on top of their payments to maintain a good credit score. Missing payments can lead to late fees and damage your creditworthiness. They need to create a budget to track spending and ensure they have enough funds to cover debt obligations each month. A business should consolidate high-interest unsecured debt into a lower-interest loan to make repayment more manageable. Negotiate with creditors if you're struggling to make payments to see their willingness to work out a payment plan or settle for a reduced amount.

A Note to be taken from all of this: all types of debt have their advantages. They all require careful management to avoid financial pitfalls.

HOW DEBT AFFECTS YOUR COMPANY'S FINANCIAL HEALTH

To say there is no positive effect of debt on a business is just not true. Debt can be a valuable tool for companies looking to expand their operations or invest in growth opportunities. When you take on long-term debt, you can secure the funds needed to acquire assets, fund capital projects, or even facilitate mergers and acquisitions. These strategic moves can lead to increased profitability over time, as leveraging debt allows you to grow your business and generate higher revenues. What this means is that debt can catalyze long-term financial success that can propel your company toward sustainable growth and prosperity.

However, the negative impact of debt on a business is what can be regarded as more profound.

NEGATIVE EFFECTS OF DEBT ON YOUR BUSINESS

FINANCIAL STRAIN

A notable drawback of accumulating high levels of debt is the financial strain it imposes on your company. As interest expenses mount due to borrowing, the company's net income can be significantly impacted, leading to reduced profitability.

This can create a cycle where a large portion of your company's earnings is diverted towards servicing debt rather than being reinvested in the business or distributed to shareholders. Can see how destructive this is? The burden of high debt levels can hinder your company's ability to manage economic downturns or unexpected challenges, and your business's financial health can be put at risk.

INCREASED RISK

Excessive debt brings about a heightened level of financial risk. As the amount of debt increases, so does the company's financial leverage. It amplifies the potential consequences of unfavorable events. If the company struggles to meet its debt obligations, it may face consequences such as credit rating downgrades, increased borrowing costs, or even bankruptcy. Moreover, high debt levels can make it challenging for your company to secure additional financing or respond flexibly to changing market conditions. That further exacerbates your financial vulnerability.

RESTRICTED FINANCIAL FLEXIBILITY

High levels of debt can restrict a company's financial flexibility by limiting its ability to pursue new opportunities or adapt to evolving circumstances. When a significant portion of your company's cash flows is allocated towards debt repayment, there is less room to invest in research and development, expand operations, or weather unexpected expenses. This reduced flexibility can impede the company's ability to innovate, compete effectively in the market, or respond swiftly to emerging trends.

AFFECTS SHAREHOLDER CONFIDENCE

Accumulating excessive debt can erode shareholder confidence in the company's financial stability and performance. Shareholders may become concerned about the company's ability to manage its debt load, meet its financial obligations, and sustain its operations over the long term. This lack of confidence can lead to a decline in the company's stock price, reduced investor interest, or even shareholder activism. Maintaining a healthy balance between debt and equity helps to foster trust and transparency with shareholders, and their continued support and commitment to the company's growth objectives.

Assessing your ability to repay debt obligations, evaluating interest expenses, and ensuring manageable interest rates are critical aspects of debt management.

Striking a balance between debt and equity in your capital structure is paramount. While debt can be a powerful tool for funding growth opportunities, excessive levels of debt can lead to financial instability. This is why you should carefully assess your repayment capabilities, interest rates, and the debt-to-equity ratio to determine the appropriate amount of debt to take on. Once you find the right equilibrium between debt and equity, you can ensure that your company remains financially robust and resilient in the face of economic challenges.

To maintain a healthy financial position, a business needs to prioritize profitability alongside debt management. Profitability serves as a key indicator of how efficiently your company generates profits from its operations. Regardless of the amount of debt your company carries, strong profitability can bolster your financial health and stability.

One measure commonly used to evaluate your company's long-term sustainability is the debt-to-equity (D/E) ratio. A lower D/E ratio signifies that a larger portion of your company's operations is funded by shareholders rather than creditors. This lower risk of defaulting on debt obligations can enhance your company's reputation with creditors and investors, showcasing a robust financial position.

MONITORING DEBT-TO-EQUITY (D/E) RATIO

When assessing your company's long-term sustainability, one important metric to consider is the debt-to-equity (D/E) ratio. This ratio reflects the proportion of a company's operations financed by shareholders versus creditors. A lower D/E ratio signifies a higher level of financial stability, as it indicates that shareholders are contributing more to the company's capital structure. This can be viewed favorably by creditors, showcasing a reduced risk of default on debt obligations.

The following are some key points to consider regarding debt-to-equity ratio:

1. A lower D/E ratio indicates a stronger financial position and reduced risk of default.
2. Creditors may view a company more favorably with a lower D/E ratio.
3. Striking a balance between debt and equity is necessary for maintaining financial stability and sustainability in the long run.

Keeping the D/E ratio in check allows you to demonstrate responsible financial management and mitigate the risks associated with excessive debt.

IMPORTANCE OF PROFITABILITY

A profitable company is better equipped to weather economic downturns, seize growth opportunities, and attract investors who value stability and consistent returns.

A company with high profitability can withstand challenges posed by debt and maintain a strong financial standing. It indicates the ability to cover expenses, repay debts, and still generate earnings for future growth. Without solid profitability, your company may struggle to meet debt obligations. And that means that they risk financial instability and potential default.

Understanding the relationship between profitability and debt is, therefore, important for making informed financial decisions in business. The company with low profitability and high debt levels may face difficulties in sustaining its operations. It may struggle to generate sufficient cash flow to meet interest payments and repay principal amounts. Whereas a company with strong profitability can manage its debt effectively, ensuring financial stability. Profitability acts as a buffer against the risks associated with debt as it safeguards your company's financial health.

Improving operational efficiency, cost management, and revenue generation boosts profitability. These efforts can not only strengthen your company's financial position but also increase its ability to service debt obligations.

CONCLUSION:

Debt can have both positive and negative effects on your company's financial health. It can be a powerful tool for fueling growth and expansion, but it also carries risks that must be carefully managed.

Debt is not inherently good or bad – it's all about how you use it to drive your business forward. The golden rule is to always approach it with caution and a clear plan for repayment.

(For companies there are more types of debt to do with there listing on some type of stock market like SENIOR DEBT (or SENIOR NOTES) but this will be in my new book about the stock markets.in 2025-2026)

BUILD A FINANCIAL INFRASTRUCTURE

The financial infrastructure will put you in a position where you can get all the things done to get financial independence.

First start out with the mindset that you want to own the system and not be part of operating it, so for example your pension instead of paying premium to a company you now pay your own pension company.

Why would you do that? There are more reasons to do so, and some are subject to rules in different jurisdictions or countries. Just imagine your own pension company it gives you the Pease of mind that the money is really there, now you can make money with your pension to invest it and double it or even more if you choose the right investments, and that's not all you can generate a passive income out of it and the cost are (not everywhere) deductible from the tax.

To own your infrastructure can be a big asset as well the pension fund is part of the business structure and therefore an asset and it can make your company investible at the same time.

And there is more you can hang under this "umbrella or infrastructure" like your mortgage or insurance's and even your health care insurance.

Why have this infrastructure? It gives you more control and freedom, but it can even benefit you instead of paying others and let them make a profit you can take that back and invest these profits to build your own wealth.

Building a financial infrastructure is a multifaceted venture that requires investment knowledge and technology, ensuring accurate reporting, managing data collection, and establishing policies and controls.

This section I will go over a few areas of your business that you can focus on when building your (financial) Infrastructure:

HUMAN CAPITAL

Continuous professional development ensures that your employees stay ahead of industry trends and best practices, when the workforce within the company has the best work ethics and skills they become an asset to the company as well.

TECHNOLOGY

Innovative technologies like automation streamline financial processes, reduce errors, and enhance operational efficiency. Do you know you can ensure seamless financial operations simply by assessing and consolidating payment processing systems and billing platforms? Leveraging cloud-based solutions helps you to stay agile and adapt to changing market conditions with ease. There are numerous program options like insurance reporting systems or private wealth systems that can be run beside the accounting software od you can integrate it with each other.

ACCURATE REPORTING

Establishing reliable access to data and determining the types of reports needed for making informed decisions. Internal reporting offers insights into your business's financial performance, while external reporting fosters transparency with share and stakeholders, it will also function as a benchmark for investors, insurance companies and banks if they need to invest in your company.

DATA COLLECTION

Effective data collection and management is also very important to avoid data integrity issues that can compromise decision-making. You can implement robust systems for collecting, storing, and distributing financial data. But ensure data quality, integrity, and security is at the highest level. Leveraging data management tools like data warehouses and analytics solutions empowers you to derive valuable insights from your financial data. Consistent data collection from various sources enables a comprehensive view of your financial status.

POLICIES AND CONTROLS

Documenting policies and controls ensures that financial transactions are carried out in a structured and consistent manner, reducing the risk of errors. So, implementing internal controls like authorization processes and regular audits provides assurance that your financial operations align with regulatory requirements.

LEVERAGING TECHNOLOGY & INNOVATION

Technology & innovation enhance operational efficiency and also help your team to adapt to market changes swiftly. Assessing and consolidating your payment processing systems and billing platforms ensures a seamless flow of financial operations.

WHAT CAN TECHNOLOGY DO FOR YOU?

Harnesses the Power of Cloud Solutions: Cloud-based solutions can offer unparalleled flexibility and scalability in managing your financial infrastructure. When you leverage cloud technology, you can access real-time data, streamline collaboration, and improve your decision-making processes.

The cloud provides a more secure and centralized platform for storing and analyzing financial information and helps you to make data-driven choices with confidence. So, working with this technology empowers your organization to respond effectively to market dynamics and drive sustainable growth.

Automates Financial Processes: Automation is a key driver of efficiency in financial operations. It not only reduces the risk of human error but also accelerates the speed of financial transactions. For efficiency in your financial operations, automate routine tasks such as data entry, reconciliation, and reporting. Doing that will help you free up valuable time for your team to focus on strategic initiatives.

Enhances Operational Resilience: Incorporating technology into your financial infrastructure enhances operational resilience and business continuity. This can be achieved by using cutting-edge tools and systems to mitigate risks, improve compliance, and respond proactively to market challenges. Technology enables you to adapt quickly to changing regulations and industry trends - it ensures that your financial operations remain robust and adaptable.

RISE OF DIGITAL PAYMENTS

The emergence of digital payment channels and mobile technologies has revolutionized the way we conduct financial transactions. A company that takes advantage of digital payment infrastructure will be able to process payments more efficiently, reduce costs, and reach a broader customer base. This shift towards digital payments fosters financial inclusion by providing access to financial services in underserved areas. It also drives economic growth and facilitates international trade.

Digital payments have the ability to expand market reach. Digital payment solutions enable businesses to tap into international markets, overcome currency barriers, and facilitate cross-border transactions. This expansion of market reach often increases revenue opportunities and enhances the customer experience. The result is loyalty and trust among stakeholders.

To enhance transparency, security, and trust in financial operations, a business should consider working with blockchain technology and distributed ledger systems.

API INTEGRATION AND OPEN BANKING

API integration and open banking are revolutionizing the way businesses interact with financial institutions and share data securely. By leveraging

Through Application Programming Interfaces (APIs), companies can collaborate with third-party service providers to offer personalized financial services and streamline platform integration. This kind of collaboration will enhance customer experience and bring about innovative financial products to meet ever-changing market demands.

Open banking, fueled by API integration, enables individuals and businesses to access a wider range of financial services and products, and it empowers consumers with more choices and flexibility. Through secure data sharing, financial institutions can provide tailored solutions that cater to specific customer needs.

A company that buys into this idea will eventually enjoy increased customer satisfaction and loyalty. The seamless exchange of data between systems promotes efficiency and transparency in financial transactions, which benefits both businesses and consumers alike.

The adoption of API integration and open banking fosters a more connected and interoperable financial ecosystem, where diverse financial services can seamlessly interact to meet consumer needs. For instance, by breaking down traditional barriers and silos, businesses can offer a more holistic and integrated financial experience, which enhances convenience and accessibility for their customers.

The ability to integrate with a diverse range of financial providers and services opens up new avenues for growth and innovation, positioning businesses at the forefront of the evolving financial landscape.

EXPLORING B-TO-B LENDING AND DECENTRALIZED FINANCE (DEFI)

If you are intrigued by the concept of Business-to-Business lending and decentralized finance (DeFi), it should be because the platforms offer transparent, open, and permissionless financial services that can revolutionize the way you manage your finances.

With B-to-B lending, businesses can access loans without traditional financial institutions. And that promotes financial inclusion and expands lending opportunities.

Business-to-Business lending platforms operate on the principles of trust, transparency, and efficiency.

They cut out the middleman and streamline the lending process connecting borrowers directly with lenders. This direct interaction fosters a sense of community and collaboration, which creates a more personalized and efficient borrowing experience.

With DeFi, smart contracts (used with the system) automate transactions to guarantee security and reliability without the need for intermediaries. The decentralized nature of DeFi platforms provides users with greater control over their financial assets. Through blockchain technology, transactions are executed securely and transparently. The goal is to reduce the risk of fraud and manipulation.

Smart contracts enable automated processes, such as lending and borrowing, without the need for traditional financial institutions. It's a decentralized approach that empowers individuals to take control of their finances and explore new opportunities for wealth creation.

DOUBLE-ENTRY BOOKKEEPING

The double-entry bookkeeping system is widely used in the world and acts as a world standard and works with the Debit – Credit system.

Double entry accounting reduces errors and boosts the chance of your books balancing. Your company can benefit from using Double entry bookkeeping because, not only reducing errors, but it also helps with financial reporting and prevents fraud.

One of the main reasons that Double entry bookkeeping is so accurate is that it implements the "matching principle". The matching principle makes sure that expenses relate to revenue. Recording both means you're accurately calculating profit and loss.

One of the main reasons that Double entry bookkeeping is so accurate is that it implements the "matching principle". The matching principle makes sure that expenses relate to revenue. Recording both means you're accurately calculating profit and loss.

Human error can disrupt your company's financial position. Double entry bookkeeping reduces the chance of this as it provides checks and balances. Errors can easily be found with Double entry bookkeeping because the debit and credit amounts are equal. Although errors are greatly reduced, it does not mean that it will entirely prevent all errors.

Double entry bookkeeping reduces fraud /errors by leaving an audit trail. Audit trails allow you to trace transactions that are posted in the general ledger. For example, if your bank balance seems too high on your balance sheet, you can trace back the transactions made to the bank account and see if they're accurate.

Financial statements are easy to prepare if your company uses Double entry bookkeeping because info is gathered directly from the Double entry bookkeeping transactions in the system. It's important for companies to produce accurate financial statements efficiently quickly and on time. Management depends on financial statements to keep an eye on the company's performance financially and to create budgets. But also stake holders, like investors, banks, depend on financial statements to view a company's creditworthiness.

As I mentioned above keeping accurate records within your company is crucial to running a professional and "investible" company. To be able sell your company later to big investors they need to be able to track everything they need to do their due diligence.

WHY MAINTAIN ACCURATE FINANCIAL RECORDS?

Double entry bookkeeping reduces fraud /errors by leaving an audit trail. Audit trails allow you to trace transactions that are posted in the general ledger. For example, if your bank balance seems too high on your balance sheet, you can trace back the transactions made to the bank account and see if they're accurate.

What are the top benefits of maintaining accurate financial records?

TRANSPARENCY AND ACCOUNTABILITY

In accounting, transparency, and accountability are paramount for establishing credibility and trust with external stakeholders and regulators. When presenting your financial reports to financial institutions and potential investors, transparency and accountability are often regulated and should also be a priority within the business.

DETAILED RECORDING

Accurate financial records ensure that every financial transaction has is trackable within the system (General ledger). It provides a clear trail of a company's financial activities. With both debit and credit entries documented for each transaction, stakeholders can easily trace the flow of funds and find the underlying data.

CLEAR UNDERSTANDING

Accurate financial record keeping allows banks/financial institutions and investors to audit your financial records with a level of certainty. If a company supplies a detailed account of its financial position, it has shown its commitment to openness and clarity in its accounting practices, and this resonates well with investors especially. Everyone is well informed about what is happening in the organization.

INTEGRITY

Good financial records signal to external parties the level of professionalism within your company and the level of integrity. This level of professionalism not only instills confidence but also reduces the perceived risk for lenders and investors and can strengthen your company's creditworthiness in the eyes of others.

DETECTION OF ERRORS

Any company that wants to remain relevant for long must maintain accurate and reliable financial statements to assure external stakeholders, financial institutions such as banks, investors and so on, that the information presented is trustworthy and free from material misstatements. It must adopt the culture of tracing transactions and verifying the accuracy of financial data. This is especially necessary where discrepancies or anomalies arise. If it fails to position itself as trustworthy and reliable in the eyes of banks and potential investors, it may crash with time.

ACCURACY

If you adhere strictly to the principles of double-entry bookkeeping, you can ensure the accuracy of your financial records. This precision will not only help in the enhancement of the transparency of your company's financial position, but it will also help you build trust with banks and investors.

RELIABILITY

The historical reliability of double-entry bookkeeping as an industry standard gives credibility to any financial reporting. Banks and investors are more likely to trust companies that follow established accounting practices like the principles of double-entry bookkeeping.

CONSISTENCY

Consistent use of double-entry bookkeeping demonstrates your commitment to sound financial management practices. Consistency signals to external stakeholders that your company values accuracy, transparency, and accountability in its financial dealings.

VERIFICATION

The verification process inherent in double-entry book-keeping allows for easy detection of errors or discrepancies. A business that actively reconciles its accounts by ensuring that debits and credits agree, can present an error-free financial picture to any bank or investor.

So, how can you improve financial reporting within your company, knowing that the importance of accurate and reliable data cannot be overstated?

Double-entry bookkeeping serves as a foundation for improving financial reporting within a company. With it, companies can be sure that their financial statements are based on solid and consistent data, and this often supplies a comprehensive representation of their financial health. It, in turn, instills confidence in banks and potential investors who rely on these reports to make informed decisions.

The strict practice of double-entry bookkeeping enhances the accuracy of financial statements through what is called “the matching principle.” The principle ensures that expenses are accurately matched with revenue to give a more precise calculation of profit and loss. That means that companies can present financial reports that reflect a true picture of their financial performance.

The implementation of double-entry bookkeeping reduces the likelihood of errors in financial reporting.

With checks and balances inherent in the system, discrepancies or mistakes can be easily identified and rectified. It both contributes to the overall reliability of the financial statements of your company and minimizes the risk of inaccuracies that could undermine the company's credibility with external parties.

In practice, there are unique reasons why companies adhere to the double-entry bookkeeping principles like:

BUILDING CREDITWORTHINESS/ACCESS TO FAVORABLE FINANCING OPTIONS

The practice of double-entry bookkeeping is not just a mundane task of recording numbers; it is a powerful tool that can significantly impact a company's creditworthiness.

When your company practices double-entry bookkeeping, it opens the door to a lot of favorable financing options. Banks and investors are more inclined to offer competitive loan terms and investment opportunities to companies with transparent and accurate financial records. And don't forget access to favorable financing options is needed for sustaining and expanding your business operations.

With a solid financial foundation built on accurate records and industry-standard practices, you are better positioned to negotiate favorable terms that support your growth and development objectives.

Moreover, the trust and confidence instilled by double-entry bookkeeping can enhance your company's reputation in the eyes of financial institutions and investors. When external stakeholders perceive your company as creditworthy and financially stable, they are more likely to view your business as a reliable and low-risk investment opportunity. This positive perception can lead to increased interest from lenders and investors.

ENHANCED FINANCIAL ACCURACY

Practicing double-entry bookkeeping suggests that you are interested in elevating your company's financial accuracy to new heights. This is because accounts remain balanced and error-free when you record every transaction with both a debit and a credit entry.

This approach reduces the risk of financial discrepancies and provides a transparent view of your company's financial health.

BETTER DECISION-MAKING

The structured nature of double-entry bookkeeping empowers you to make informed decisions based on reliable financial data. This doesn't sound strange as accurately recording your revenues, expenses, assets, and liabilities helps a business to gain valuable insights into their level of performance and profitability. It also enables them to identify trends, analyze variances, and strategize for future growth.

STRENGTHENED INTERNAL CONTROLS

As noted earlier, double-entry bookkeeping requires dual entries for every transaction just to create checks and balances that help prevent errors and detect fraud. The segregation of duties and the reconciliation of accounts further enhance the security and integrity of your financial records. As a result, you can trust in the reliability of your financial data and safeguard your company against potential risks and uncertainties.

STREAMLINED FINANCIAL REPORTING

Double-entry bookkeeping streamlines your financial reporting processes and makes it easier for your team to prepare accurate and timely statements.

With all financial transactions meticulously recorded and categorized, you and your team can quickly generate comprehensive reports that reflect your company's financial performance.

This efficiency not only saves time and resources but also ensures that your financial statements comply with industry standards and regulatory requirements.

THE WORKING SYSTEM EXPLAINED.

For a lot of people, the accounting world is a lot of Abra-ca-Dabra, to give you an insight into the working system behind the double entry bookkeeping system I have summed up some of the basics.

DEBIT ON THE LEFT, CREDIT ON THE RIGHT

One of the fundamental rules is to place debits on the left and credits on the right. This simple principle ensures that each transaction is carefully documented and reflects the true financial state of a business.

The principle states, “debit receives the benefit, credit gives the benefit.” This concept at its core emphasizes the exchange of value in financial transactions.

When an account is debited, it signifies that the entity or account is receiving the benefit of the transaction. On the contrary, a credit entry indicates that the entity or account is providing the benefit in the transaction.

Imagine a scenario where a company purchases raw materials from a supplier on credit. In this case, the company’s inventory account is debited as it receives the benefit of acquiring the raw materials. But the accounts payable account is credited as it signifies the supplier giving the benefit of providing the materials. This principle ensures that every transaction is recorded to accurately reflect the give-and-take nature of financial dealings.

Ensuring Accuracy: Aadhering to the principle of “debit receives the benefit, credit gives the benefit,” helps businesses maintain a transparent record of their financial transactions. This practice upholds the integrity of the accounting process and also enables stakeholders to make informed decisions based on reliable information. The systematic application of this principle ensures that each entry in the books of accounts tells a coherent story of value exchange.

Strategic Decision-Making: understanding the dynamics of debits and credits in terms of benefits received and given allows businesses to strategize effectively. They can analyse the flow of resources through the lens of this principle. Ccompanies can optimize their financial operations, identify areas of improvement, and make sound business decisions.

FOR EVERY DEBIT, THERE MUST BE A CREDIT

"For every debit entry, there must be a corresponding credit entry," is the second principle. The principle ensures that the financial records accurately reflect the give and take of resources within the business. Without this balance, discrepancies and inaccuracies can creep into the books. That can result in financial mismanagement.

To maintain the integrity of the accounts, the concept of "balancing the books" is always going to be relevant. It pays attention to detail and ensures that every transaction is accurately captured and that the financial statements provide a true representation of the business's financial position.

Whether it's a debit to receive value or a credit to give value, the harmony between the two principles is essential for the smooth operation of the double-entry system.

FOR PERSONAL ACCOUNTS - DEBIT THE RECEIVER, CREDIT THE GIVER

When dealing with personal accounts, the principle to remember is to debit the receiver and credit the giver. This principle ensures that transactions involving individuals, associations, or firms are aappropriately recorded. By debiting the receiver, you acknowledge that they have received value, while crediting the giver signifies that they have given something of value.

In professional terms, this in principle means that when you receive money from a client, you would debit their account to reflect the increase in their balance. Conversely, you would credit your account to show that you have received funds from them.

FOR REAL ACCOUNT - DEBIT WHAT COMES IN, CREDIT WHAT GOES OUT

Real accounts focus on assets and liabilities rather than individuals. For real accounts, the principle is simple: "debit what comes in, credit what goes out." This means that any increase in assets should be debited, reflecting the inflow of resources into the business. Then, any decrease in assets, such as payments or expenses, should be credited to show the outflow of resources.

This principle will help you track the movement of your assets within your financial records. when a company purchases new machinery, the machinery account is debited to reflect the increase in asset value. But, when the company sells old equipment, the machinery account is credited to show the decrease in asset value.

The concept of debiting what comes in and crediting what goes out in real accounts is essential for maintaining the balance and integrity of financial records. This principle ensures that every transaction involving assets is accurately recorded, whether it involves acquiring new assets or disposing of existing ones. It provides a clear and systematic way to track the value of assets over time and make informed financial decisions based on accurate data.

FOR A NOMINAL ACCOUNT - DEBIT ALL EXPENSES, CREDIT ALL INCOMES

Nominal Accounts are dedicated to tracking all expenses incurred and all incomes earned during a specific period. The way (principle) to follow when dealing with them is to debit all expenses and credit all incomes. It will help you accurately assess your profitability and financial health.

When an expense is recorded in a Nominal Account, it is debited to reflect the outflow of funds from the business. Whether it's operating expenses, taxes, or interest payments, debiting expenses, by default, reveals the costs incurred to generate revenue. Now, crediting all incomes in a Nominal Account highlights the revenue generated by your business. It will not only unravel the revenue-generating activities but also aid in calculating net profits.

Balancing Nominal Accounts ensures that the company's profit and loss statement reflect a true representation of its financial activities. This balance is necessary for stakeholders, investors, and management to gauge the financial success and sustainability of a business.

UNDERSTANDING PERSONAL ACCOUNTS

Personal accounts record transactions related to individuals, associations, and firms. To ensure accurate recording of these transactions, you must understand the following:

Debit the receiver, credit the giver: When dealing with personal accounts, always remember to debit the receiver and credit the giver. This principle reflects the flow of resources between individuals or entities.

Receiver of benefits: The account that benefits from a transaction is debited, indicating an increase in its assets or a decrease in its liabilities.

Giver of benefits: The account that provides the benefit is credited, showing a decrease in its assets or an increase in its liabilities.

Be aware that each transaction involving personal accounts must have a corresponding debit and credit entry to ensure balanced books and transparent financial records.

UNDERSTANDING REAL ACCOUNTS

When it comes to real accounts in the double-entry system of bookkeeping, the focus shifts to tangible assets and liabilities that a business owns or owes. Real accounts capture the essence of the company's financial position by recording what comes in and what goes out in terms of physical assets and debts. This category includes accounts like cash, inventory, buildings, equipment, and loans.

The precision of real accounts lies in their ability to mirror the physical aspects of a company's financial dealings. From the cash flow to the physical assets and debts, real accounts must provide a comprehensive view of the company's financial status.

By debiting what comes into the business, such as cash from sales or investments, and crediting what goes out, like payments for expenses or loan repayments, real accounts provide a clear record of the company's financial transactions. This is to ensure that the company's assets and liabilities are correctly represented in the books.

If the double-entry principle is used in updating real accounts, you would be able to easily determine your company's liquidity, solvency, and general financial stability.

CONCLUSION,

Mastering (or having a expert in house or hire one) the principles of the double-entry system of bookkeeping is vital for maintaining accurate financial records. When you understand the fundamental rules of debits and credits, as well as the specific guidelines for different types of accounts, you can ensure that your books reflect a true and accurate financial status of your business.

THE FUNCTION OF A GOOD BOOK/ RECORD KEEPING SYSTEM.

To have a good functioning book/record keeping system is vital for every professional business/organisation as it is the financial lifeline.

It has multiple functions as you can trace the cash flow or the upcoming taxes and the cost of running the business and much more.

It can also help you:

1. Steer the business/organisation.
2. Make decisions on investments.
3. Make growth plans.
4. Detect Fraud.
5. Keep the company professional and investible.
6. Keep track of your Assets.
7. Keep track of Bank accounts and loan positions.
8. Keep track of your outstanding invoices.

Proper bookkeeping provides you with valuable insights into your cash flow, expenses, and general financial standing. A business that keeps accurate and up-to-date records will be in a better position to make informed decisions that drive it toward success. This is the primary purpose of proper record-keeping in any organization.

WHAT ARE THE BASIC FUNCTIONS OF GOOD RECORD-KEEPING?

COMPLIANCE AND EFFICIENT PLANNING

Proper bookkeeping helps you track your expenses, monitor your income, and ensure that you are meeting your tax obligations. When you have organized records, you can streamline financial planning processes, identify potential cost-saving opportunities, and pave the way for sustainable growth.

CASH FLOW MANAGEMENT

With proper bookkeeping, you can track your incoming and outgoing electronic payments or cash, identify patterns in your revenue streams, and proactively address any cash flow challenges. You will be able to avoid cash crunches, seize opportunities for expansion, and maintain a healthy financial position.

BETTER DECISION-MAKING

Every smart investor knows that making informed decisions is key to staying ahead of your competition. Proper bookkeeping provides you with the data and insights you need to make strategic decisions that drive your business forward. Whether it's evaluating investment opportunities, assessing profitability, or identifying areas for growth, having accurate financial records at your fingertips will always help you take calculated risks and seize new opportunities.

HOW TO ENSURE PROPER BOOKKEEPING PRACTICE

ACCOUNTING SOFTWARE

The first step is to carefully select the right tool that favors your business needs. Consider options depending on the size or level of professionalism each offers special features tailored to different business and its complexities. Take the time to evaluate their user interface, functionalities, and compatibility with your operations before making a decision.

Once you've chosen your accounting software, configure it to suit your business requirements. Familiarize yourself with the software's features and settings to ensure smooth operation. Input your company's information, including bank accounts, tax details, and financial data, to set up a solid foundation for accurate record-keeping. Customizing the software to your specific needs will streamline your bookkeeping process and enhance efficiency in managing your finances.

As you do that, don't hesitate to seek assistance from professionals, online resources, or customer support. Take advantage of training materials provided by the software provider to maximize your understanding of its capabilities. Utilize features like invoice generation, expense tracking, and financial reporting to create a seamless bookkeeping system

CHOOSE AN ENTRY SYSTEM

There are two main options in choosing an entry system for your bookkeeping: single-entry or double entry. The single-entry method is suitable for small businesses with straightforward financial transactions, while the double-entry method provides a more comprehensive approach. If you opt for a double-entry system, you can accurately track both income and expenses in the same system.

Making the decision on the entry system to use is necessary for maintaining accurate records of your business's financial transactions. With a double-entry system, you can ensure that every dollar (or your country's currency) coming in and going out is accounted for. This level of detail not only helps in tracking your cash flow effectively but provides a basis for making better financial decisions, moving forward.

Whether you opt for a single-entry or double-entry system, the golden rule is to choose one that aligns with the complexity of your financial transactions.

SELECT AN ACCOUNTING METHOD

As a business owner, selecting the right accounting method will help to accurately reflect your financial position. There are two primary methods to choose from: cash basis and accrual basis.

The cash basis method records transactions when cash is exchanged. It gives a clear picture of actual cash flow. The accrual basis method recognizes revenue when earned and expenses when incurred, regardless of cash movement. You may consult with an accountant to determine which method is best for your business needs and financial goals. The accounting method you select will have an impact on your financial reporting and tax obligations.

While the cash basis method offers simplicity and immediate cash insight, the accrual basis method provides a more comprehensive view of your business's financial health. Consider factors such as your industry, revenue recognition timing, and business structure when deciding on an accounting method.

Ensure that the method you choose accurately reflects the true financial performance of your business, to help you make informed decisions and comply with regulatory requirements.

Don't forget that accurate financial reporting reveals your business's profitability and attracts potential investors. So, when you choose an accounting method that favors your business operations, you can present reliable financial statements that will give confidence to stakeholders. Investors and lenders often look for businesses with consistent and transparent financial reporting. That is why it is imperative to choose an accounting method that accurately represents your business activities.

ORGANIZE YOUR FINANCIAL ACTIVITIES PROPERLY

Managing transactions by recording all financial activities, from production to sales and expenses, in a systematic and timely manner. Your team should always stay on top of your transactions, maintain a clear audit trail and have a comprehensive overview of your business's financial health. They may use accounting software to streamline this process and make it easier to generate invoices, track bills, and reconcile bank statements.

STAY DILIGENT IN DOCUMENTING TRANSACTIONS

Accuracy is key when it comes to managing transactions. Make sure to diligently document every sale, purchase, expense, and payment. This helps in maintaining accurate records, as well as helps in identifying potential areas for cost optimization. With a well-organized system in place, you can easily track your financial activities, monitor cash flow, and make smarter decisions to drive your business forward into a new future, and ensure a log lasting solid business.

EMBRACE AUTOMATION FOR EFFICIENCY

Accounting software can automate repetitive tasks like generating invoices, tracking payments, and sending reminders to customers. Use them to save time and resources so that you can focus on growing your business. Keeping on top of non-paying customers can save you a significant amount of money on a yearly basis.

MONITOR CASH FLOW CLOSELY

Effective transaction management also involves monitoring cash flow closely. Keeping a watchful eye on your incoming and outgoing funds helps your business remain financially healthy. Understanding your cash flow patterns can help you make strategic decisions, such as when to invest in growth opportunities or how to optimize expenses.

SEEK PROFESSIONAL GUIDANCE (WHEN NEEDED)

If you find yourself overwhelmed with managing transactions, don't hesitate to seek professional guidance. Accountants or financial advisors can offer useful insights and expertise to help you handle complex financial matters. Working with them will ensure that your transactions are accurately recorded, compliance requirements are met, and financial goals are achieved. Don't hesitate to reach out for assistance when needed to ensure the success of your business. It will cost you only a few bucks if you compare it to the expensive mistakes otherwise made.

HANDLE ACCOUNTS RECEIVABLE AND PAYABLE

Handling accounts receivable and payable involves ensuring timely payments from customers and managing obligations to suppliers with finesse. Efficiently managing accounts payable equally secures financial stability and vendor relationships.

Establish clear invoicing and payment policies to streamline the collection of outstanding invoices.

Automated invoice generation, payment tracking, and reminders to maintain a smooth cash flow process.

Monitor accounts receivable to promptly address any overdue payments and maintain positive customer relations.

Set clear payment terms with suppliers to avoid late fees and maintain a good rapport.

Utilize accounting software features to track and manage accounts payable, ensuring bills are paid on time.

Communicate proactively with suppliers to address any payment issues promptly and maintain a harmonious business relationship.

WORK WITH A TAX SPECIALIST

Tax regulations can be complex and ever-changing. This is why you need a professional by your side. Working closely with a tax specialist ensures that your business remains compliant with all tax requirements, minimizes tax liabilities, and takes advantage of tax-saving opportunities. A tax specialist can provide valuable insights into tax deductions, filing requirements, and strategies to maximize tax savings for your business.

A tax specialist is not just a consultant but a strategic partner in your business's financial success.

Working with a tax professional will help you focus on growing your business while leaving the tax intricacies to the expert. It's a win-win situation that sets your business up for long-term success and sustainability. Their expertise can help you optimize your tax planning strategies and avoid costly mistakes.

CONCLUSION,

Setting up accounting software, choosing an entry system, selecting an accounting method, and managing transactions effectively will give you a peace of mind in knowing that your financial records are accurate and up to date. Handling accounts receivable and payable, setting up payroll, and coordinating with a tax specialist will also help you manage complex financial matters with ease.

Good bookkeeping practices not only protect your business from potential risks but also provide valuable insights for making informed financial decisions. So, the importance of maintaining a solid bookkeeping system has more than one function within your business.

CHAPTER THREE

STOCK MARKETS

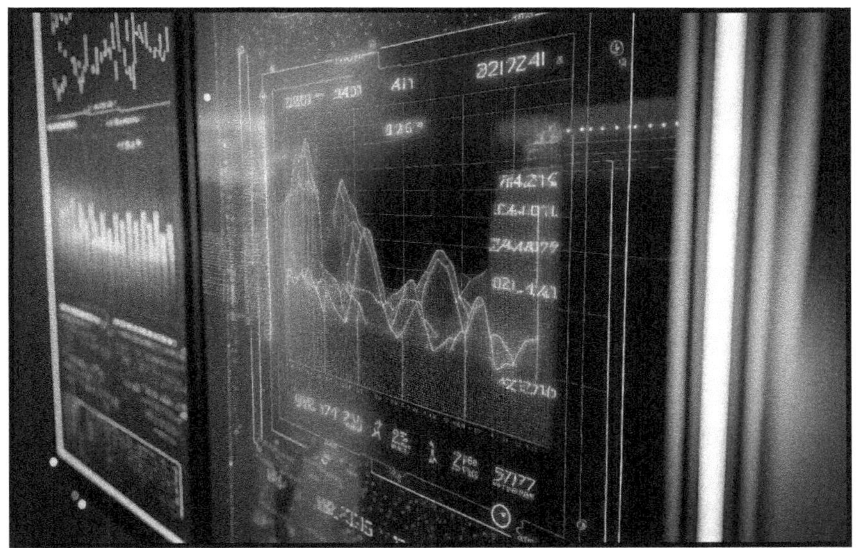

Have you ever wondered how companies raise capital, investors grow their wealth, and economic performance is measured? The stock market is responsible for these. The stock market is a complex system that drives global economies and offers opportunities for investors to grow their wealth.

Your company as an entity is divided in stocks the total of these stocks is the value of the business and it can have separate owners. (shareholders or stake holders) and it can be divided into several levels like a stock with voting rights or non-voting stocks and there are much more variants.

The company needs to have a record of the owners of these stocks in the register of shares and allotment journal.

When a company starts an IPO (Initial Public Offering) it will offer the shares to the public for the first-time through a stock issuance and creates opportunities for the company to attract new capital from investors.

WHAT ARE THE FUNCTIONS OF THIS MARKET?

FACILITATING CAPITAL FORMATION

A primary function of the stock market is to act as a conduit for companies to raise capital.

When a company decides to go public through an Initial Public Offering (IPO), it offers shares to the public and attracts new capital from investors. By selling shares, a company can secure funds to fuel its growth, expand operations, or undertake strategic initiatives. This process of capital formation both benefits the company and provides opportunities for investors to participate in the success and growth of businesses.

PROVIDING LIQUIDITY AND INVESTMENT OPPORTUNITIES

Through the stock exchange, investors can easily buy and sell shares. That is, they can convert their investments into cash with relative ease. This liquidity ensures that investors can swiftly adjust their portfolios, seize investment opportunities, or divest from underperforming assets. Also, the stock market offers a diverse range of investment opportunities that allow investors to diversify their holdings across different sectors, industries, and asset classes to manage risk and maximize returns.

ESTABLISHING MARKET VALUATIONS

Publicly trading shares makes companies subjected to market forces that determine the price of their stocks based on supply and demand. This process of price discovery reflects investors' perceptions of a company's value, growth prospects, and financial performance. Market valuations not only influence stock prices but also serve as a barometer of market sentiment, economic conditions, and industry trends.

STIMULATE ECONOMIC GROWTH AND DEVELOPMENT

Beyond individual companies and investors, the stock market contributes to broader economic growth and development. As companies raise capital on the stock exchange, they have the financial resources to innovate, create jobs, and drive economic prosperity.

The stock market acts as a catalyst for entrepreneurial ventures, enabling businesses to access funding and pursue ambitious projects that stimulate economic activity. Through the facilitation of investment and capital formation, the stock market helps sustain economic growth, fostering innovation, and shaping the future of industries and markets.

WHO ARE THOSE THAT CONTRIBUTE TO THIS MARKET?

Here are some of the key players you will encounter in the stock market:

Individual Investors: These are everyday people like you who invest in stocks through brokerage accounts to build wealth or save for the future.

Institutional Investors: This category includes pension funds, mutual funds, and insurance companies that manage large pools of money on behalf of clients and shareholders.

Once you can recognize the varied participants involved in the market, you gain insight into the diverse motivations and goals that drive investment decisions. It doesn't matter whether you're a novice investor or a seasoned pro, you need to have an understanding of the different market participants to make informed choices in the stock market.

UNDERSTANDING SECURITIES AND EXCHANGES

Securities such as stocks and bonds reign supreme in the stock market. Stocks represent ownership in a company. Stocks grant shareholders voting rights and a stake in corporate profits. On the flip side, bonds are debt instruments issued by entities to raise capital. Both assets are the lifeblood of the stock market because they are used to fuel investment opportunities and financial growth.

While stocks and bonds are the assets traded, stock exchanges are the platforms where these assets are bought and sold. These exchanges, like the New York Stock Exchange (NYSE), Nasdaq and Russel 2000 and more, provide the infrastructure for companies / commodities to list their shares for public trading. Investors can choose to buy shares of public companies listed on various stock exchanges, diversifying their portfolios and capitalizing on market fluctuations.

THE REGULATORY FRAMEWORK IN THE STOCK MARKET

Regulatory bodies like the Securities and Exchange Commission (SEC) are saddled with the responsibility of upholding integrity and fairness in the stock market. The SEC oversees stock exchanges, brokers, financial advisors, and mutual funds to safeguard investors' interests and ensure transparent markets. Through stringent enforcement of securities laws, the SEC maintains a level playing field where fraudulent activities are investigated, and compliance is rigorously monitored.

Having a clear-cut understanding of the regulatory framework in the stock market is necessary to safeguard your investments and ensure a level playing field for all market participants. The SEC upholds ethical standards and enforces regulatory guidelines - it creates a conducive environment for fair and transparent trading.

WHAT ARE MARKET INDICES?

Market indices are like barometers of the overall market performance, which measure the value of a specific section of the market. The most popular indices, such as the S&P 500, Dow Jones Industrial Average, and Nasdaq Composite, track the performance of different types of stocks and give investors a snapshot of how the market is doing.

Market indices help investors gauge market trends, compare investment performance, and make informed decisions about their portfolios. Many of them try to keep an eye on these indices to stay ahead of market movements and adjust their investment strategy accordingly.

INVESTORS OR STAKEHOLDERS

Investors and stakeholders are the driving forces behind any company's operations and their decision-making processes. While often used interchangeably, they each bring unique perspectives and roles to the table. Each and every one has their distinct relationship with a company.

Although investors are also stakeholders, the term 'stakeholder' encompasses a broader scope - it includes employees, customers, suppliers, communities, and more people in your industry.

While investors focus on financial returns and direct capital allocation, stakeholders encompass a broader range of interests that shape the company's decisions and impact on society.

Investors: Investors are individuals or entities who provide capital to the company with the expectation of a return on their investment (ROI). They engage in economic transactions directly with the business, such as purchasing stocks or bonds, to fuel the company's growth and success. Their primary focus is on financial returns and maximizing the value of their investment within the company's operations.

Stakeholders: Stakeholders are parties with an interest in the company, who can influence or be affected by its activities. They include diverse individuals and groups, such as employees, customers, suppliers, communities, governments, and trade associations. While some stakeholders may overlap with investors, stakeholders are not solely driven by financial gains. Their interests extend beyond profits alone to encompass various social, environmental, and ethical concerns within the company.

Level of Involvement: While investors focus on financial returns / the structure of the company and may actively steer strategic directions, stakeholders bring a diverse range of other perspectives and interests to the table.

Investors: Investors have a financial stake in the company, which directly ties their level of involvement to the company›s growth / product/ internal structure and also the success or failure. Their engagement is targeted at maximizing their return on investment (ROI) and therefore closely monitor the company's performance and its strategic decisions. As significant shareholders or members of the board of directors, investors may actively participate in key decision-making processes to safeguard their interests.

Stakeholders: Stakeholders can have a varied scope of interests. While they may not have a direct financial stake in the company like investors do, they are still impacted by the company›s actions. Stakeholders can include employees, customers, suppliers, communities, and even activist groups with different perspectives. Their level of involvement may differ based on their relationship and role within the company.

INTERESTS AND OBJECTIVES

Investors seek opportunities for value creation and monitor closely the (financial) performance and stakeholders advocate for social and environmental sustainability. These differentials of priorities can sometimes create tension but can also result in a balanced approach that considers and empowers both financial and non-financial factors.

Companies that can effectively navigate and align these divergent interests are often more resilient and sustainable in the long run.

When a company engages with stakeholders and incorporates their feedback into decision-making processes, it can build trust, enhance reputation, and foster a culture of accountability and transparency. This collaborative approach not only benefits the company, there stake and shareholders but also contributes to the community.

Investors: will focus on returns and maximizing the value of their investments. Their main goal is to add value to the company as well as protect and grow their capital and influence.

Stakeholders: Stakeholders have another spectrum of interests. For instance, employees may prioritize fair wages and working conditions, while customers seek high-quality products and services.

ROLES OF INVESTORS IN A COMPANY

CAPITAL ALLOCATION

Investors often make available the necessary funds for the growth and development of a business.

Here's how they contribute to this aspect of a company's operations:

Enabling Growth: Investors provide the capital needed for businesses to invest in infrastructure, research and development, marketing, and other key areas. This financial support is needed for a company›s expansion and success.

Facilitating Innovation: With the backing of investors, businesses can explore innovative ideas, products, and services that drive progress and competitiveness in the market.

Supporting Strategic Initiatives: Investors can help companies execute strategic initiatives by providing the financial resources required to implement new projects, enter new markets, or optimize existing processes.

Fueling Long-Term Success: Investors can also contribute to the long-term sustainability and growth of a company through the effective allocation of resources. This creates value for both the organization and its stakeholders.

Shareholder Activism: Shareholder activism is a powerful tool wielded by investors who hold substantial shares in a company. These proactive shareholders push for positive changes within the organization through various means. As they start proposing resolutions, engaging in proxy voting, and advocating for corporate governance practices that match their values, they influence a company's direction and decision-making processes significantly. Shareholder activism serves as a catalyst for driving growth, enhancing transparency, and fostering accountability within the company.

Shareholder activism is not merely about voicing concerns or demanding change; it is about actively participating in the company's governance and decision-making processes. Investors who engage in shareholder activism often conduct thorough research and analysis to identify areas for improvement and propose actionable solutions.

Investors engaging in shareholder activism demonstrate a commitment to guiding the company towards sustainable practices and ethical standards. Through their active involvement and advocacy, they seek to improve the company's operational efficiency, governance structure, and performance and therefore add value to the company. Also, by leveraging their influence and shareholder rights, these investors can help shape a company's strategic direction and ensure that it remains aligned with the interests of all stakeholders involved.

The impact of shareholder activism goes beyond financial gains; it extends to promoting a culture of accountability, integrity, and social responsibility within the company. The activities of holding management accountable, advocating for sustainable practices, and driving positive change, help investors contribute and work towards a more resilient, ethical, and transparent corporate environment. Their efforts not only benefit the company but also create a ripple effect that positively impacts the broader business community and society.

Financial Performance: Ideally, investors can analyze financial statements, performance indicators, and market trends to assess the company's profitability and growth potential. They can closely track these metrics to make informed decisions about their investments and influence a company's strategies.

Investors' interest in financial performance also extends to influencing the company's resource allocation. Through their analysis and evaluation of financial data, investors can provide valuable insights and recommendations to help improve the company's financial health and long-term sustainability. They engage with the company's management team and board of directors to advocate for sound financial practices, transparent reporting, and effective risk management strategies. Such a collaborative approach between investors and company leadership can lead to improved financial performance and value creation for all stakeholders.

Conclusion: Both investors and stakeholders contribute towards the success of every business. An investor is a type of stakeholder, focused on capital allocation and shareholder activism, driving financial performance and long-term value creation. (so called Value Investors)

Meanwhile, a stakeholder (when they are not particularly an investor) has a different relationship with a company, they either work for the company or are involved in many other ways.

RISK CALCULATION

Taking risk is invadable in the world of doing business but if we can keep this within certain boundaries and protect your capital at the same time it will be a win-win.

First step is to calculate or get a reasonable insight what the upside will be for the business and is it long term or short-term risk.

When estimating the opportunity and cost associated with the decision you need to:

1. Identify the choices that are open in the deal.
2. Identify what resources are available and will (or can) be used.
3. Are the resources available within the business or do you need external capital?
4. The sum of the opportunities and the economic value versus the cost and pressure on the resources (internal or external) of the deal will determine if you do the deal or not.

To look at risk in a radical way can be very helpful in taking difficult decisions you can take the upside versus the downside (see chapter 4) and take all the knowledge in consideration.

In this section I will walk you through different approaches and methodologies so you can make informed decisions within your risk calculations.

Likelihood x Severity Formula for Risk Calculation: Calculating risk in business is like solving a complex puzzle, where each piece represents a potential threat to your company's success. One widely used approach in risk assessment is the Likelihood x Severity formula. This formula serves as a compass that guides you through the treacherous waters of uncertainty by quantifying the probability of a risk occurring and the magnitude of its impact. By multiplying the likelihood of a risky event by its severity, you can gauge the overall impact that risk may have on your business.

Picture it as a mathematical equation, where the variables of likelihood and severity converge to give you a comprehensive view of the potential risks looming on the horizon and beyond.

To apply the Likelihood x Severity formula effectively, you must first identify and analyze the different risks your business may face.

You have to assign a numerical value to both the likelihood and severity of each risk so that you can plug these values into the formula to calculate the overall risk score. Think of it as conducting a risk calculation as in aviation or before a space flight (also consider working with check lists), dissecting each potential threat to understand its probability and impact. Armed with this data, you can prioritize risks, allocate resources efficiently, and develop robust mitigation strategies to protect your business from potential harm.

(Keep in mind that the Likelihood x Severity formula is not just a theoretical concept it is a practical tool that can help you make sound decisions in the face of uncertainty.)

THE PROCESS FOR CALCULATING RISK IN BUSINESS

Follow these steps to effectively calculate risk:

Identify and define the kinds of risks: Start by categorizing and defining the various types of risks that your business may encounter. For things like financial uncertainties, operational challenges, market fluctuations, or regulatory hurdles, formulate a risk matrix that will give a clear roadmap for risk assessment.

List actions that impact risk levels: Now, identify the actions or activities that could either amplify or mitigate risks. Why is this necessary? When you understand how different decisions and processes can influence risk levels, you can proactively manage uncertainties and capitalize on opportunities.

Assign a rank to each action: Once you›ve listed the actions affecting risk, prioritize them based on their level of impact. High-risk actions demand closer scrutiny and more frequent review, while low-risk activities can be monitored with a lighter touch. This ranking system will guide your risk management efforts toward areas that require immediate attention and mitigation strategies.

How to Create a Scatterplot of Risk: One effective method to visualize and analyze risks is by creating a scatterplot. This visual representation allows you to plot the variables of risk and probability - it gives a clear snapshot of potential correlations.

When creating a scatterplot of risk, the first step is to gather relevant data points that encompass various risk factors. These data points could range from financial metrics to market trends, each contributing to the overall risk profile of your business. When you collect and organize this data, you lay the groundwork for a comprehensive analysis that reveals areas of both high and low risk.

Once you have compiled the necessary data, plot the variables on your scatterplot. Each point represents a special combination of risk and probability. This approach gives a visual representation of the risk outlook. Through this graphical depiction, you can easily identify patterns, outliers, and trends that might not be apparent in raw data alone. You need this step to gain a holistic understanding of the risks facing your business.

As you analyze the scatterplot, pay close attention to areas of high and low-risk concentration. By pinpointing clusters of high-risk points, you can prioritize your risk management efforts and implement targeted strategies to mitigate potential threats. Conversely, areas of low risk can provide insights into areas of strength and opportunities for growth. Armed with this knowledge, you can make better decisions that protect your business's future, even in the face of uncertainty.

Oke now, how do you analyze areas of high and low risk?

If you are not strategic here, you will mess the whole thing up. You need to examine the data and trends to pinpoint where potential risks may arise and where opportunities lie. It's like being your own detective, uncovering hidden clues that can shape your decision-making process. This analytical mindset helps you to proactively address high-risk areas before they escalate, while also capitalizing on low-risk areas for growth and expansion.

Visualizing the risk through a scatterplot can give valuable insights into the correlation between risk and probability. This process involves connecting the dots between various risk factors and their potential impact on your company's performance. It's akin to solving a complex puzzle, where each piece represents a different risk element that must be carefully examined and evaluated.

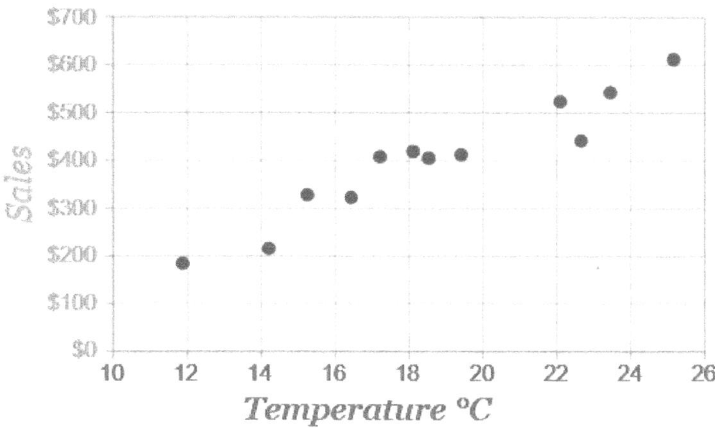

Example of a scatterplot.

PROFIT SEGMENTATION AND TRANSACTION-BASED METRICS FOR RISK CALCULATION

By dissecting the profit of a company, you can identify areas of strength, weakness, and untapped potential for strategic risk management. The fusion of profit segmentation and transaction-based metrics revolutionizes the way businesses approach risk calculation.

A company needs to fortify its financial foundations and weather the storms of uncertainty. This is why it must prioritize profit peaks, mitigate profit drains, and address potential profit deserts. This granular analysis secures profitability and sustainability.

In tandem with profit segmentation, transaction-based metrics offer a magnifying glass into risk calculation. Scrutinizing every invoice line through the lens of profit and loss will help your company gain a nuanced understanding of the impact of individual transactions on profitability.

A company that applies the Likelihood x Severity formula and follows a structured process in calculating risk can effectively assess and manage its risks to make informed decisions. Incorporating profit segmentation and transaction-based metrics will also provide it with valuable insights into the financial implications of its risk management strategies.

SHARES AND THE COMPANY STRUCTURE

Shares are more than just pieces of paper or an electronic blip. They represent a stake in the ownership of a company. Whether held by founders, investors, or employees, the distribution of shares shapes the ownership structure of a company. Different types of shares come with distinct rights and privileges, such as voting rights, dividend entitlements, and conversion options. As a shareholder, you hold an important position within the company, with rights and responsibilities that influence the direction and performance of the business.

TYPES OF SHARES

There are common shares, preferred shares, and convertibles. Common shares grant voting rights and potential dividends, preferred shares offer priority in dividends and assets, and convertible shares provide flexibility for investors.

As a shareholder, the type of share you hold determines your rights and responsibilities within the company.

Common shareholders will have the privilege of voting on critical matters, such as the election of directors, while preferred shareholders may enjoy a fixed dividend rate and priority in receiving dividends and assets. Knowing the nuances of shareholders' rights and responsibilities guides you in participating in a company's governance.

WHAT ARE THE RIGHTS AND RESPONSIBILITIES OF A SHAREHOLDER?

As a shareholder, you are not just a passive investor; you hold an important role in the company's decision-making process. (if you have stocks with voting rights)

Here are some key rights and responsibilities that come with being a shareholder:

Voting Rights: Most common shares will grant you the right to vote on important company matters, such as the appointment of directors or major strategic decisions. Your voice matters in shaping the direction of the company.

Dividend Entitlement: Depending on the type of shares you hold, you may be entitled to receive dividends, which are a portion of the company's profits distributed to shareholders. This can be a rewarding aspect of being a shareholder.

Information Rights: You have the right to access certain company information, such as financial reports and annual statements. This transparency ensures that you can make informed decisions about your investment.

Responsibility for Liabilities: While you are generally not personally liable for the company›s debts beyond your initial investment, you still have to understand the potential risks and responsibilities that come with being a shareholder.

TYPES OF COMPANY STRUCTURES

There are different types of company structures. Each offers unique advantages and challenges that shape a business' effectiveness.

Functional/Role-Based Structure: The functional or role-based structure is a traditional organizational framework characterized by clear hierarchies and specialized functions. Clear accountability and specialization are key features of this structure. They are needed because they promote efficiency and expertise within specific departments. However, limited cross-functional collaboration may pose challenges in fostering innovation and adaptability across the organization.

Product or Market-Based Structure: In a product or market-based structure, the organization is organized around specific products or market segments. It enables a deep focus on customer needs and tailored strategies for each product or market. Its advantages include efficient resource allocation and product/market focus. It has its drawbacks too. For example, potential duplication of functions across divisions may hinder synergy and increase costs.

Geographical Structure: The geographical structure organizes the company based on geographic regions or locations. It facilitates a localized approach to operations and customer engagement. But, with this structure, coordinating activities across geographies and maintaining consistency in operations can be challenging.

NOW, WHAT ARE THE ADVANTAGES OF ADOPTING EACH OF THESE STRUCTURES?

Functional/Role-Based Structure: In a functional/role-based structure, clarity reigns supreme. Each employee has a distinct role within the organization, reporting to a specific manager or supervisor. This clear delineation of responsibilities promotes accountability and streamlines decision-making processes. By knowing exactly who is responsible for what, employees can focus on their specialized functions.

Specialization and Expertise: The role-based structure, employees are grouped based on their specific functions. Individuals can develop expertise and excel in their respective areas. In the areas of finance, marketing, operations, or human resources, employees can hone their skills and contribute their specialized knowledge to the overall success of the organization. This depth of expertise can lead to innovation and competitive advantage in the marketplace.

While the functional structure excels in promoting specialization, it may encounter challenges in fostering cross-functional collaboration. Communication and coordination between departments may become strained, hindering organizational agility and adaptability.

Finding ways to bridge the gaps between different functions and encourage collaboration can be key to maximizing the potential of a functional structure and driving innovation through diverse perspectives.

HOW CAN YOU ACHIEVE THIS?

Break Down Silos for Effective Communication: To overcome the limitations of limited cross-functional collaboration, breaking down silos will be helpful. Encouraging open communication channels between departments, promoting cross-team projects, and fostering a culture of sharing knowledge and ideas can help bridge the divide. Try to create opportunities for employees to work across functional boundaries so that your organization can leverage the diverse expertise within the team, and spark creativity and innovation.

Balance Specialization with Collaboration: It is true that the functional structure offers the benefits of expertise and efficiency, but it is advisable to cultivate a culture of collaboration and teamwork.

If you combine the strengths of specialization with the power of cross-functional collaboration, you can unlock new possibilities, drive innovation, and adapt to changing market demands.

Product or Market-Based Structure: When critically checked, the Product or Market-Based Structure stands out as a strategic framework tailored to companies with diverse product lines or operating in multiple markets. This organizational structure aligns departments or divisions based on specific products or markets. This enables a laser-focused approach to meeting customer needs and crafting customized strategies for each product or market segment. It fosters a deep understanding of consumer demands.

Key characteristics of your Product or Market-Based Structure include efficient resource allocation, where resources are strategically directed towards individual products or markets. This deliberate allocation ensures that resources are utilized effectively. It often results in heightened customer satisfaction and enhanced operational performance.

One potential challenge of your Product or Market-Based Structure lies in the risk of duplication of functions across different divisions or departments. The duplication can lead to increased costs, reduced synergy between teams, and potential inefficiencies in resource utilization.

Companies adopting this structure must be careful in streamlining processes, fostering interdepartmental collaboration, and ensuring clear communication channels to lessen the risks associated with duplicated functions.

Geographical Structure: Geographical structure organizes a company based on geographic regions or locations and allows for a more localized approach to operations. The structure can enhance communication, adaptation to local market needs, and efficient resource allocation. The aim of this structure is to optimize a company's global presence and leverage regional strengths for sustainable growth.

CONCLUSION.

Understanding the different company structures and shares is a must for anyone who wishes to invest in any business. With such knowledge at your disposal, you will be well-equipped to make informed decisions that drive the growth and prosperity of your business or secure the investment needed, as the case may be.

RISK-ADJUSTED RETURN ON CAPITAL (RAROC)

Risk-Adjusted Return on Capital or (RAROC) is a tool that can be useful in assessing potential acquisitions. The assumption of RAROC is that investment projects with higher levels of risk mostly offer substantially higher returns.

If your company or organisation needs to compare different projects must keep this assumption base in mind.

RAROC is also often referred to as profitability-measurement framework (based on the risk side)

This allows your analyst to examine a company's financial performance and give an Insite and stabile view of profitability across business sectors and industries. This will also help you form a better investment plan for the short and long therm.

Risk-Adjusted Return on Capital (RAROC) is a financial metric that is widely used in measuring the profitability of a business while taking into account the associated risks. RAROC looks at both factors simultaneously to give an overview of how effectively your business is utilizing its capital. This metric is often needed to decide where to allocate resources and how to manage risks efficiently.

To calculate RAROC, you divide the net income generated by your business activities by the economic capital required to support those activities. This calculation yields a percentage that reflects the returns your business is generating relative to the amount of capital at risk. The ratio will help you assess the profitability of different investments or projects and determine the optimal capital allocation strategy for your business.

The risk-adjusted return on capital (RAROC)is calculated as follows:

- Risk-adjusted return on capital = (Revenues – costs – expected losses) / Economic capital

In this example the RAROC for the bank but you can adjust this to your own situation.

Revenue is the bank revenue in the form of transaction fees and interest collected. Borrowers are charged interest for borrowing money. The interest and fees the bank collects cover the various costs it incurs, such as operational and financing costs.

The **expected loss** is the predicted loss of the business based on industry averages. This is considered the risk of loss and is recovered from borrowers in the form of a risk premium. The formula for expected loss is:

Expected loss (EL) = Probability of default (PD) * Loss given default (LGD) * Exposure at default (EAD)

For the NON-Banking organizations RAROC is used as a metric for the effect that there operational, market and credit risk have on their finances.

COMPONENTS OF RAROC

All of the components below work together to provide a comprehensive view of your financial performance while considering the associated risks:

Expected Returns: Expected returns encompass a range of factors, including revenue, expected losses, expenses and income generated from capital. To quantify the expected returns accurately, evaluate the revenue streams and costs associated with your business activities. This analysis allows you to determine the net income generated and assess the financial viability of your projects. This process enables you to make informed choices about where to allocate your resources. It will help you optimize capital deployment.

Risk Adjustment: In the context of RAROC, risk adjustment involves assessing the risk profile of each investment or business unit to determine the appropriate returns that should be generated. This component recognizes that higher levels of risk should come with the potential for higher returns. It reflects the fundamental relationship between risk and reward in investments. When you factor in the level of risk associated with each investment or business unit, there will be a more accurate assessment of profitability.

Risk adjustment considers various factors such as market risk, credit risk, and operational risk to provide a clear picture of the risks involved. It helps organizations to better understand the trade-off between risk and return.

Capital Allocation: Capital allocation is an aspect of financial management that involves distributing your company's capital across various business units or investments based on their risk-adjusted returns. This strategic approach allows businesses to prioritize investments that offer the highest potential returns relative to the associated risks. Through capital allocation, you can make informed decisions on where to allocate more capital to achieve your business goals.

Generally, the goal of effective capital allocation is to maximize profitability while managing risks prudently. By optimizing how you allocate capital across your business units or investments, you can enhance your financial performance and generate sustainable returns for your stakeholders.

IMPORTANCE AND APPLICATIONS OF RAROC

Here are some key reasons why RAROC is significant:

Quantifies Risk: Risk-Adjusted Return on Capital (RAROC) is a powerful tool to quantify the risks associated with your investments or projects.

RAROC can help determine if your business activities are generating sufficient returns given the level of risk present. This metric both highlights the potential returns from your investments and considers the level of risk you are exposed to. With RAROC, you can optimize your capital allocation by directing more resources toward ventures with higher risk-adjusted returns.

Guides Business Decisions: Instead of relying on gut feelings or vague estimations, you can leverage RAROC to compare different options and select those that offer the highest risk-adjusted returns. When you do this, you can adopt a more data-driven and analytical approach to investment evaluation. It helps you to assess the profitability of various projects in a systematic manner, taking into account both the expected returns and the inherent risks involved.

Therefore, the application of RAROC in your decision-making process will help you strategically deploy your capital where it can generate the best returns while managing risks effectively.

Optimizes Capital Usage: A key benefit of using RAROC to optimize capital usage is the ability to prioritize investments based on their risk-adjusted returns. It makes you concentrate on your capital where it will have the most impact. That enhances your financial performance and strengthens your risk management practices for a more resilient and successful business model.

Enhances Risk Management: RAROC prompts key decision-makers in a company to identify potential risks associated with investments or business activities and implement strategies to mitigate them.

The holistic view of profitability provided by RAROC ensures that risk management is not treated in isolation but is considered in conjunction with financial performance. Organizations can make well-informed decisions that balance profitability with risk exposure.

With RAROC as a guiding metric, businesses can enhance their overall risk management practices and fortify their resilience in the face of challenges.

Does RAROC have limitations? Yes, it does. RAROC relies on assumptions and estimates, which can introduce a level of subjectivity into the analysis. It may also not account for all types of risks, such as operational or regulatory risks, which could impact on the accuracy of the results. Is important to consider these limitations when using RAROC to make decisions about investments and projects.

Understanding Risk-Adjusted Return on Capital (RAROC) can empower you to make more informed decisions about capital allocation and risk management within your business.

Every business owner needs it to optimize capital usage, enhance risk management, and make strategic decisions with confidence.

CALCULATING RAROC EXPLAINED

COMPONENTS OF THE RAROC FORMULA:

Revenue: Revenue represents the income generated by your investment, including transaction fees and interest collected. You have to calculate the total revenue earned from your investment activities to determine the financial viability of your venture.

Expenses: Expenses include all the costs associated with your investment, such as operational and financing costs.

Expected Loss: Expected Loss is an important component of the RAROC formula, as it accounts for the predicted loss based on industry averages. When you consider the probability of default, loss given default, and exposure to default, you can assess the risk associated with your investment and adjust your strategies accordingly.

CALCULATING EXPENSES:

Expenses directly impact on your bottom line and need to be carefully considered when evaluating the financial health of your investment. It is good to break down your expenses into categories to get a comprehensive view of where your money is being allocated.

Whether it's fixed costs like rent for buildings or other assets or variable costs like production cost or labor cost, a detailed breakdown of expenses will provide valuable insights into the financial performance of your project. This detailed analysis can help you identify potential cost-saving opportunities and make strategic adjustments to enhance your investment's returns.

Direct expenses are those costs that can be specifically attributed to the project, such as materials for production and so on or labor costs. On the other hand, indirect expenses are costs that are incurred for the overall operation of your business but are not directly tied to the project, such as administrative expenses. Accounting for both direct and indirect expenses help to paint a more accurate picture of the financial health of your investment and make well-informed decisions based on this data.

Calculating Expected Loss: Expected Loss represents the average loss you can anticipate over a specific period. By evaluating Expected Loss, you can better comprehend the financial impact of potential defaults or losses within your investment portfolio.

This metric serves as a key factor in determining the risk-adjusted profitability of your investments.

Several factors influence the calculation of Expected Loss, including historical data, industry trends, and credit risk assessments. Statistical models and probabilistic methods are commonly used to predict Expected Loss accurately.

You need to also factor risk assessment techniques into the calculation of Expected Loss to enhance the precision and reliability of your financial analysis. Leveraging credit ratings, market conditions, and other relevant factors will help refine your Expected Loss estimates and strengthen your risk management practices. These techniques enable you to adapt to changing market dynamics and anticipate potential challenges.

Calculating Capital: Capital, in this context, refers to the amount of money or assets that have been invested in the project or investment. It is the basis upon which the potential returns and risks are built.

Calculating the capital invested will help you assess the level of resources you have dedicated to the investment and evaluate whether the returns are commensurate with the amount invested.

To calculate the capital, you need to consider all the financial resources that have been allocated to the project. This includes the initial investment, additional capital injections, and any retained earnings that have been reinvested back into the project.

In addition to assessing the financial aspects, calculating the capital also enables you to gauge the risk exposure of the investment. The amount of capital invested directly influences the level of risk undertaken in the project. A higher capital investment signifies a greater exposure to risk, as more resources are at stake. It will help you evaluate the risk-return trade-off and determine whether the potential returns justify the risks involved.

Now, capital charges, which represent the cost of capital, are used in determining the general profitability of the investment. Considering capital charges in your calculation helps you ascertain the return that investors expect for investing in the project and gauge whether the returns are sufficient to cover these costs. This insight is needed for making decisions about the viability and sustainability of the investment.

Calculating Income from Capital: In determining the income from capital for your investments, you must consider the capital charges and the risk-free rate. Here's how you can calculate this component of the RAROC formula:

The income from capital is obtained by multiplying the capital charges by the risk-free rate.

Capital Charges: This represents the cost of capital or the return that you expect for investing in a particular project. It is needed to factor in the opportunity cost of tying up your funds in the investment.

Risk-Free Rate: The risk-free rate is the rate of return on an investment with zero risk. It is derived from government bonds or other low-risk investments and serves as a benchmark for the minimum return you should expect.

Calculating the income from capital will help to evaluate the risk-adjusted return on your capital investments and can guide you in making informed financial decisions.

CONCLUSION.

Understanding and utilizing the Risk-Adjusted Return on Capital (RAROC) and Expected Loss metrics can be invaluable in assessing the profitability and risk of your investments. You can gain a comprehensive view of how well your investments are performing in relation to the associated risks. This knowledge can empower you to make informed decisions about your financial endeavors. That leads to more successful investment strategies.

RETURN ON RISK – ADJUSTED CAPITAL (RORAC)

Risk-Adjusted Return on Capital or (RAROC) is a tool that can be useful in assessing potential acquisitions. The assumption of RAROC is that investment projects with higher levels of risk mostly offer substantially higher returns.

If your company or organisation needs to compare different projects must keep this assumption base in mind.

RAROC is also often referred to as profitability-measurement framework (based on the risk side)

This allows your analyst to examine a company's financial performance and give an Insite and stabile view of profitability across business sectors and industries. This will also help you form a better investment plan for the short and long therm.

When it comes to measuring return on capital adjusted for risk, both Return on Risk-Adjusted Capital (RORAC) and Risk-Adjusted Return on Capital (RAROC) are go-to metrics. While RAROC focuses on adjusting the return for risk, RORAC takes a different approach by adjusting the capital for risk. This distinction is needed because it emphasizes the importance of firm-wide risk management in evaluating projects and investments.

RORAC VS. RAROC: WHAT SETS THEM APART?

Understanding the difference between RORAC and RAROC will guide you in your decision-making process. RAROC, as the name suggests, adjusts the return for risk, aiming to provide a clearer picture of the risk-adjusted profitability of a project. On the other hand, RORAC adjusts the capital for risk.

With the inclusion of risk-weighted assets into the calculation, RORAC offers decision-makers a standardized and comprehensive metric to assess projects with varying risk profiles. This enables a more accurate comparison of projects and allows for a better understanding of their performance and profitability.

THE IMPORTANCE OF RORAC

In financial analysis, Return on Risk-Adjusted Capital (RORAC) holds significant importance for decision-makers.

The below explains why this metric is important for evaluating projects and investments effectively:

Apples-to-Apples Comparison: RORAC enables a standardized comparison of projects with varying risk levels. It considers the capital at risk and provides an accurate assessment of a project's performance.

Comprehensive Measure of Return: Unlike traditional return on capital metrics, RORAC takes into account the risk associated with the capital investment. This measure of return provides a more general view of a project›s profitability. And that guides decision-makers in resource allocation.

Enhanced Risk Management: By placing a strong emphasis on firm-wide risk management, RORAC encourages organizations to approach risk assessment strategically. Different corporate divisions can utilize RORAC to quantify and maintain acceptable risk-exposure levels.

EVALUATING PROJECTS BASED ON RORAC

This is a practical example to grasp the significance of Return on Risk-Adjusted Capital (RORAC) in evaluating projects.

Imagine you have two projects, Project A and Project B, each with different financial metrics. Project A generates a net income of $1,000,000, while Project B boasts a higher net income of $2,000,000. However, when we consider the risk-weighted assets, Project A has $10,000,000 and Project B has $20,000,000. These figures lay the basis for a comparative analysis using RORAC.

Calculating the RORAC for each project will help you understand their performance relative to the capital at risk.

For Project A, the RORAC is calculated as follows:

- Net Income ($1,000,000) divided by Risk-Weighted Assets ($10,000,000) - which equals 0.1 or 10%.
- Similarly, for Project B, the RORAC calculation yields the same result of 10%.
- Despite Project B having a higher net income, the RORAC metric allows us to see that Project

A is more efficient in generating returns based on the capital at risk.

- The beauty of RORAC lies in its ability to offer a fair comparison of projects with varying risk levels. Decision-makers can make informed choices about resource allocation and investment opportunities simply by considering the capital at risk in the analysis.
- In our case study, Project A demonstrates the importance of efficiency in generating returns, showing how RORAC can provide valuable insights into project performance beyond revenue figures alone. The case study highlights the practical application of RORAC in evaluating projects based on the capital at risk.

Analysis of Project A: Project A is a prime example of how Return on Risk-Adjusted Capital (RORAC) can reveal the performance of a project based on the capital at risk. With a net income of $1,000,000 and risk-weighted assets of $10,000,000, Project A shows a RORAC value of 10%. This metric provides a standardized measure of the project's efficiency in generating returns considering the level of risk involved.

Calculating the RORAC for Project A allows you to see how effectively the project utilizes the capital at risk to generate income. By dividing the net income by the risk-weighted assets, you obtain a straightforward percentage that reflects Project A's performance. This enables decision-makers to make informed choices regarding resource allocation and investment opportunities.

Analysis of Project B: Let's shift our focus to Project B, which presents a different set of numbers but holds equal importance in the realm of financial evaluation. With a higher net income of $2,000,000, Project B shows its potential for generating substantial returns. However, this project also comes with higher risk-weight assets amounting to $20,000,000. This juxtaposition of higher revenue and higher risk underscores the need to go deeper into the numbers to uncover the true efficiency of Project B.

CALCULATING RORAC FOR PROJECT B

The calculation is straightforward yet insightful:

RORAC equals net income divided by risk-weighted assets.

With a net income of $2,000,000 and risk-weighted assets of $20,000,000, Project B's ORAC value is 0.1

or 10%. This percentage serves as a pivotal indicator of Project B's efficiency in utilizing the capital at risk to generate returns.

Deciphering the Significance: The parity in RORAC values between Project A and Project B underscores the importance of a comprehensive evaluation framework. While revenue figures may sway initial perceptions, RORAC delves deeper into the efficiency of projects in generating returns based on the capital at risk. This nuanced approach to financial analysis enables decision-makers to make informed choices regarding resource allocation and investment opportunities, paving the way for strategic decision-making in a dynamic financial landscape.

ANALYSIS

Here's a breakdown of the analysis:

Project A: Despite having a lower net income compared to Project B, Project A shows a RORAC of 10%. This indicates that Project A is more adept at generating returns based on the capital at risk, making it a more efficient investment choice.

Project B: Project B boasts a higher net income than Project A, but also a RORAC of 10%. While Project B may have higher revenue figures, its efficiency in generating returns based on the capital at risk is on par with Project A.

Key Takeaway: The takeaway or analysis of these projects underscores the significance of RORAC in evaluating investments. RORAC considers the capital at risk through risk-weighted assets and provides a fair comparison of projects with varying revenue figures but similar levels of risk. This allows decision-makers to make informed choices regarding resource allocation and investment opportunities.

Conclusion, the analysis of Project A and Project B exemplifies how RORAC can offer a comprehensive insight into the performance and efficiency of investments. Utilizing RORAC as a metric will help decision-makers make strategic investment decisions based on a standardized method of evaluating projects.

WHAT ARE THE LIMITATIONS OF RORAC?

Complexity: One limitation is the complexity involved in calculating risk-adjusted capital. The process requires a deep understanding of the company›s risk profile and the appropriate weighting factors for different assets, making it challenging to implement RORAC consistently across various projects and organizations.

Inherent subjectivity: Another limitation to consider is the subjectivity inherent in the risk assessment process. Assigning weights to different assets involves judgment and analysis, which can introduce bias and inconsistency in the calculation of RORAC. This subjectivity may impact the reliability of the metric, and it raises concerns about the accuracy of the evaluation.

Lack of standardization: With no universally accepted method for determining RORAC, variations in approach across organizations can arise. This lack of standardization makes it difficult to compare RORAC values between companies or industries, hindering the ability to benchmark performance effectively.

Despite these limitations, it is important to recognize that RORAC remains valuable for evaluating projects and investments. RORAC provides decision-makers with a more comprehensive measure of return on capital. It enables a fair comparison of projects with different risk profiles, and so cannot be done away with at any time.

In conclusion, understanding RORAC can help you make informed decisions regarding investment opportunities, as it considers both the potential return and the associated risk.

Through the comparison with RAROC and the case study provided, you can see how RORAC provides a clearer picture of project performance, allowing for more accurate assessments. However, it is essential to acknowledge the limitations of RORAC, such as its reliance on assumptions and the potential for overlooking qualitative factors.

CAPITAL TO RISK WEIGHTED ASSET RATIO OR CAPITAL ADEQUACY RATIO

One of the most important financial ratios that analysts and investors use to measure the available capital in percentage of the risk-weighted credit exposure.

It is also known as “the capital adequacy ratio”.

Under accounting standards like Basel III the banks have a minimum requirement of the capital-to-risk weighted asset ratio of 10.5%, by having these worldwide standard it gives a stable and also efficient financial system, it also leaves an audit trail as well to be able to check all the calculations when producing financial statements / reports.

THE FORMULA FOR THE CAPITAL-TO-RISK WEIGHTED ASSET RATIO IS:

Capital-to-risk weighted asset = Tier 1 capital + Tier 2 capital -/- Risk Weighted asset

-/- = divided by.

Tier 1 capital is the core capital of the bank, this capital includes equity and disclosed reserves. Tier 2 capital is supplementary capital that is less secure than Tier 1. A bank's risk-weighted assets are its assets weighted by their riskiness used to determine the minimum amount of capital that must be held to reduce its risk of insolvency. These items can all be found on a company or bank›s financial statements.

The capital-to-risk weighted assets ratio will help determine whether or not a bank has enough capital to take on any losses before becoming insolvent and losing depositor funds.

Banks are regulated under the Basel rules, your company does not need to comply with these rules but if you create a system within your company that automatically involves this kind of "Back up" facilities you have a safety net and audit trail to look back on if needed.

It also provides you with extra management information for you to steer the company or make better decisions.

NET ASSET VALUE (NPV)

So' What is Net Asset Value?

Net Asset Value is the value of an entity's assets minus the value of its liabilities (or more basically your assets minus liabilities) it's mostly used for funds or investment trusts.

Per- Share NAV can be seen as the price that the shares of the entity are listed for with the SEC and so the NAV can change on a daily base as the share price does.

The difference between the common share price is that this reflects the analyses of the price per share of the entity while the NAV reflects the total value of the entity minus the liabilities on all assets.

NET PRESENT VALUE (NPV) AND WHY IT IS IMPORTANT.

Net Present Value discounts a project's future net cash flows at a required rate of return it then deducts its initial cash outlay.

The (NPV) is important as it can find a current value of a future stream of payments using a proper discount rate, (NPV) also shows the time value of (currency) money or can be used to compare rates of return of several different projects.

The Net Present Value calculation is also referred to as Discounted Cash Flow (DCF) it is a widely used method to compare the NPV of a company's future DFCs with the current price, one of the big names who uses this calculation is Warren Buffet.

POSITIVE NPV AGAINST NEGATIVE NPV

The positive NPV indicates that projected earnings generated by a project or investment "discounted for their present value" exceed the anticipated costs. It is also assumed that an investment with a positive NPV will be profitable.

The investment with a negative NPV however will result in a net loss. This concept is the basis for the net present value rule, which tells us that only investments with a positive NPV should be considered.

WHY IS NET PRESENT VALUE (NPV) SO IMPORTANT?

Money or Currency you have in hand at this moment in time is probably more valuable than when collected in the future, the fact is that if you can invest it now to make money or you have to wait until (when?) it comes in and either you lost the investment opportunity or your money is depreciated and thus you need more to do the same investment.

To compare the value of money (currency) now with the future value this is where Net Present Value (NPV) can give you the insight you need to take informed financial decisions.

Net present value allows businesses and investors to assess the profitability of a project or investment, taking into account the cost of capital and the expected rate of return.

By discounting future cash flows against their present value, NPV helps businesses or investors making informed decisions, ensuring that the undertaken projects contribute to the overall financial health and growth.

RETURN ON NET ASSETS (RONA)

The return on net assets (RONA) ratio, a measure of financial performance, RONA measures how well a company's fixed assets and net working capital perform in terms of generating net income.

Return on net assets is commonly used for capital-intensive companies and is an important ratio looked at by investors to determine how effective a company is at generating a profitable return on its net assets.

FORMULA FOR CALCULATING (RONA)

The formula for calculating RONA is as follows:

$$\text{Return on Net Assets} = \frac{\text{Net Income}}{\text{Fixed Assets} + \text{Net Working Capital}}$$

Return on net assets is used to assess the financial performance of a company in relation to their fixed assets and net working capital. Like the return on assets ratio, a higher RONA rate indicates a higher level of profitability.

There is no ideal measurement to return on net assets ratio numbers, but a higher ratio is most preferable. It is important to compare the RONA of a company to rival companies. For example, a company with a RONA of 30% may look good in your own books, but that figure may actually appear poor when compared to an industry benchmark of let's say 60%.

An increasing RONA is of course desirable, as it is an indicator of improving profitability and financial efficiency.

CHAPTER FOUR

TIME FOR MONEY AND THE LIMITATION OF THE 24-HOUR DAY.

When you have a job your basically swapping time for money, as you do so you have another problem "TIME" there is only 24 hours in a day, and you also need your sleep.

This limitation is not existing when you are an owner or boss of an structure or company, within these entities you can extend your "Time" over and over again there is no limit when you think about this because every time you get close to having a limit you ether hire a person or hire another company to do the work but you still get the benefits of the income stream.

But there is more to consider like the Time Value of Money (TVM) concept, this basically means that a sum of money is worth more now than in the future due to its earning potential.

From a investor point of view for example the money can earn more today in a savings account earning interest and over time when the interest is added to the principal making even more return with compound interest.

Like delayed payments to your company is a missed opportunity for your organization, as it lacks the funds NOW to act on deals / marketing or development of new products.

The Time Value of Money (TVM) also has more than one formula's to calculate some different variants of (TVM). For this book I will only show the base calculation for Future Value.

The following formula for (Future Value):

- *PV* is the value at time zero (present value)
- *FV* is the value at time *n* (future value)
- *A* is the value of the individual payments in each compounding period
- *n* is the number of periods (not necessarily an integer)
- *i* is the interest rate at which the amount compounds each period
- *g* is the growing rate of payments over each time period

The future value (*FV*) formula is:

$$FV = PV \times [\ 1 + (i / n)\ ]^{(n \times t)}$$

TAKING ON LIABILITIES / GOOD DEBT / BAD DEBT.

When mixing up assets with liabilities you will have the intention to keep on signing up to liabilities and having the believe you acquire assets and or wealth.

To clarify if someone has a job / income paying 150.000 a year, they most likely have the intention to sign up for a mortgage and car loans phone contract and so on because they think the income of the job will pay for it, and it does UNTILL… it doesn't .. you lose your job or get a divorce …or fall badly ill… what to do?

You get a new job that pays even better than you can take on more debt and go on that long wanted holyday.

Looks good but that's not the smartest way to be managing your finances, so how to assess liabilities?

It all seems obvious, but you need a backup plan if one income stagnates at least you have an alternative this is why companies have multiple income streams or Omni-Channelling as we say. This Omni-Channelling gives you the flexibility to work independently and have your own strategies towards the markets your company's operate within.

GOOD DEBT.

What is good debt and is having debt a good thing well it can be in the business world it is a normal thing to have debt, but it has to be managed in a smart and professional way.

To start do not have any debt in your own personal name, if you have a company (LLC / LTD / BV or GMBH or other structures) these entities have limited liability, and it also means it's not your personal liability it rests within the company, therefore the company is exposed to the risk but having said so the company is also limited liability and therefore has a less exposure than a person.

BAD DEBT.

If you use debt to buy (assets) with no income it will become bad debt as in the end it only ends up being a liability.

This does not mean that the purchases are not a household asset but that is a different asset class and companies do not work with this type of asset class.

The main reason for a debt to become a bad debt within the business world is if the owner takes on the debt for the company at personal title and so taking on all the responsibilities of the debt in person. When things go wrong for whatever reason (you) in person will become insolvent.

USE DEBT TO LIFT YOUR BUSINESS.

Use “GOOD” debt to boost your business/investments this way you make the borrowed money back (with the passive income and interest) and you own the Asset outright in the end and have the passive income free for future investments or as income for you as an owner or your business.

CALCULATING DOWN SITE COMPARED TO UPSIDE.

When calculating a down site or up site keep in mind why you need to do this, it gives you a good perspective of what you really can achieve and how big the risk is.

When you look at risk it always has a downside and an upside, but what is the real risk?

The big question is how much exposure I have when things go wrong or putting it simple “How much can I Lose” when things go wrong.

So, the "Down" side will be your maximum loss, but the upside can be "unlimited" and if that is the case you have a minimum risk scenario.

This unlimited upside can be a business you purchase that has a huge growth potential and is very popular, now when properly managed you have no limitation to make as much out of this acquisition as possible.

Ther are of course a thousand ways to make a Buck and to maximize your potential so always look around what can work for you and your situation.

ECONOMIC VALUE ADDED (EVA)

The majority of business owners would agree that understanding financial performance is critical, many find concepts like Economic Value Added (EVA) confusing.

In this chapter I will explain of what EVA is, how to calculate it, and most importantly - how it can guide decisions to **increase company value**.

I will start with the simple definition of EVA and walk through the easy formula example.

INTRODUCTION TO ECONOMIC VALUE ADDED (EVA)

Economic Value Added (EVA) is a financial metric that measures your company's economic profit after accounting for the cost of capital.

EVA shows how much true economic value your company generates compared to the capital invested in the business.

Unlike traditional accounting measures like net income or earnings per share, EVA provides a more accurate report of a company's profitability and ability to create shareholder value.

EVA AND ITS KEY COMPONENTS:

The formula for EVA is:

EVA= NOPAT – CAPITAL CHARGE

NOPAT: Net Operating Profit After Tax. It's your company's after-tax operating profit adjusted to remove any accounting distortions.

Capital Charge: Cost of capital multiplied by the capital invested. This represents the minimum return expected by the investors.

WACC: Weighted Average Cost of Capital. This estimates your company's cost of financing based on its capital structure.

Invested Capital: All capital that is invested and working in your business, including equity, debt, accounts payable, etc.

Capital Structure: It is the mix of debt and equity that your company uses to finance its operations and/or assets.

If you subtract the capital charge, EVA will show the true economic profit earned above and beyond what investors could expect to earn elsewhere at comparable risks involved.

EVA differs significantly from common accounting metrics, here are a few differences:

- EVA accounts for balance sheet items like invested capital and financing costs. Metrics like EPS (Earnings per share) manly focus on the income statement.
- EVA adjusts for accounting distortions caused by things like FIFO/LIFO inventory valuation, depreciation methods, etc.

- EVA also considers the opportunity cost of capital based on investors required rate of return. Accounting profit only looks at a company's actual cost of debt or dividends.
- And so, EVA provides a much more accurate picture of the true economic profitability and shareholder value generation within your company.

CONCLUSION:

EVA is a powerful metric for assessing your company's true profitability and ability to generate value for your shareholders. Unlike other accounting measures, it accounts for the full cost of doing business (every day).

FAIR VALUE ACCOUNTING STANDARD "FAIR VALUE"

Fair value is measured by taking the asset or product's current market value and the price it was sold for by mutually agreed upon.

In the accounting "fair value standard" makes the information from the accounting more relevant, this is also known as "Mark to Market" accounting.

It's about calculating the value of the company's assets and liabilities based on there (current) market value, this then gives a more relevant look upon the accounting and how it has been categorised.

The advantage of using "Fair Value" that it is widely used in the world of accounting but also in the world of investing, as the advantages are:

- Adaptability
- Transparency on Actual income
- Accuracy
- Asset reduction

RECURRING REVENUE

The recurring revenue is that part within your company's revenue that's expected to continue in the future, these are not one-off sales but revenue streams that are predictable and have a regular interval and have a degree of certainty.

For example, prescriptions of all kind or ongoing contracts are a good example of recurring revenue also your mobile phone or streaming service on tv or other kind of contracts. And in most cases the provider will build in a cancellation fee/time if they want to quit.

Investors and other analysts will be very keen to look at this type of revenue streams also called the "Top Line" when your business has these kind of revenue streams imbedded. Investors will evaluate your company as a more reliable company and consider

Just look at this all with a conscious mind as there are no guarantees the contracts will all last indefinitely, but it will at least give much more security than none at all.

WHAT ARE INTANGIBLE ASSETS?

To define an intangible asset is not strait forward as it has many forms and can therefore be hidden out of sight but with great difference in financial impact on the business and its operation.

The intangible asset is an asset that lacks a physical presence yet holds immense value for businesses and play a pivotal role in their success and growth. It provides a competitive edge, drives innovation, and generates revenue.

The many different types of intangible assets like:

BRANDS AND GOODWILL

When we think of successful businesses, brands, and goodwill are often at the forefront of our minds. These intangible assets hold immense value and can make or break a company's reputation in the eyes of consumers.

BRANDS

A brand is more than just a logo or a name; it is the essence of a company's identity. Brands encompass the reputation, recognition, and emotional connection that consumers have with a particular product or service. Building a strong brand can foster customer loyalty, drive sales, and differentiate a business from its competitors.

GOODWILL

Goodwill is the intangible value that exceeds a company's tangible assets. It represents the intangible qualities that make a business valuable, such as customer loyalty, brand reputation, and employee morale. Goodwill can significantly impact a company's valuation and play a crucial role in its overall success in the market.

Businesses that invest in building a strong brand and cultivating goodwill can reap numerous benefits. They will have a competitive advantage, enhance brand recognition, and increase customer trust.

INTELLECTUAL PROPERTY (IP)

Intellectual property (IP) can propel any business to new heights. From patents to trademarks, IP encompasses a diverse range of intangible assets that safeguard a company's innovative creations and distinctive brand identity. Basically, with IP protection in place, businesses can confidently innovate, knowing that their ideas are shielded from imitation and replication.

The value of intellectual property extends beyond mere legal protection; it serves as a catalyst for growth and differentiation in the market. Companies that invest in developing their IP portfolio often enjoy a competitive edge, as their unique offerings captivate customers and set them apart from rivals.

It could be for a breakthrough invention or a memorable logo. If your team leverages patents, copyrights, and trade secrets, your company can monetize its creative assets, forge strategic partnerships, and expand its market reach.

SOFTWARE AND OTHER INTANGIBLE ASSETS

The software has revolutionized how companies streamline processes and enhance productivity. From project management tools to customer relationship management systems, businesses rely heavily on software to stay competitive in today's fast-paced economy. The value of software as an intangible asset cannot be overstated, as it enables businesses to automate tasks, analyse data effectively, and make informed decisions to drive growth.

CUSTOMER LISTS

In addition to software, customer lists, and proprietary methodologies are valuable intangible assets that businesses often overlook. Customer lists provide insights into consumer behaviour and preferences. It enables companies to tailor their products and services to meet market demands effectively.

PROPRIETARY METHODOLOGIES

Proprietary methodologies represent unique processes or techniques developed internally, giving businesses a competitive edge by optimizing operations and delivering exceptional value to customers.

LICENSES AND CONTRACTS

Licenses and contracts are intangible assets that can significantly contribute to a business's revenue stream. Licensing agreements enable companies to monetize their intellectual property. With them, other entities can use their patented technologies or copyrighted materials for a fee. Contracts, whether for distribution, partnership, or service provision, represent valuable agreements that can generate income and establish long-term business relationships, further solidifying a company's market position.

VALUATION METHODS FOR INTANGIBLE ASSETS

Valuing intangible assets can be a complex process due to their intangible nature. Unlike tangible assets, which can be easily appraised based on market value, intangible assets require unique valuation methods that take into account various factors.

To determine the value of intangible assets accurately, businesses often use a combination of approaches that consider the asset's income potential, market comparable, and cost of creation. They utilize three main approaches: market approach, income approach, and cost approach. Each method offers a different perspective on the value of intangible assets and helps businesses gain a comprehensive understanding of their worth.

Market Approach: This approach estimates the value of intangible assets by comparing them to similar assets that have recently been sold in the market. It analyses market data and trends; businesses can gauge the fair value of their intangible assets based on real-world transactions.

Income Approach: The income approach values intangible assets by projecting their future income-generating potential. By estimating the expected cash flows associated with the asset and discounting them to their present value, businesses can determine the value of their intangible assets based on their revenue-generating capabilities.

Cost Approach: The cost approach determines the value of intangible assets by estimating the cost required to recreate or replace them. This method considers the expenses associated with developing a similar intangible asset from scratch so that businesses can assess the value of their intangible assets based on the investment needed for their replication.

HOW DO INTANGIBLE ASSETS PROVIDE A COMPETITIVE ADVANTAGE?

A good management must understand that intangible assets are key drivers of success and differentiation. They offer businesses a unique competitive advantage that sets them apart from their rivals. How exactly do they provide this competitive edge?

Brand Power: A strong brand can create a loyal customer base, attract new customers, and command premium prices for products or services. Brands like Apple and Coca-Cola have built a reputation that goes beyond their tangible offerings. That has helped them to stand out in crowded markets and maintain a competitive edge for years.

Innovative Edge: Intangible assets like patents and proprietary technologies enable businesses to innovate and develop cutting-edge products or services. Companies that protect their innovations will stay ahead of the curve, drive market trends, and outshine competitors who lack similar intellectual property.

Differentiation: Intangible assets help businesses differentiate themselves from competitors by highlighting special qualities, values, or features that resonate with customers - patented technology, a memorable brand identity, or a proprietary process.

Customer Loyalty: Intangible assets, such as brands and goodwill, can foster strong customer loyalty and trust. When customers have a positive perception of a brand or company, they are more likely to choose it over competitors, even if prices or features are similar. This loyalty creates a sustainable advantage that translates into long-term success for the business.

IMPACT OF INTANGIBLE ASSETS ON BUSINESS GROWTH AND INNOVATION.

Proper deployment of intangible assets attracts investors and enhances the company's valuation. Investors recognize the potential for intangible assets to generate future income streams and drive profitability. Companies with valuable intellectual property, such as software or patents, are viewed favourably by investors, as these assets can translate into sustainable competitive advantages and long-term growth prospects. The presence of intangible assets can also increase the company's stock price, reflecting investor confidence in the business's ability to innovate and remain competitive.

Intangible assets not only fuel business growth but also foster a culture of innovation within the organization. Once a business owner protects their intellectual property and proprietary technologies, they indirectly encourage creativity and experimentation among their employees. This culture of innovation can also lead to the development of cutting-edge products and services, positioning the company as a leader in its industry. Intangible assets serve as a catalyst for continuous improvement and evolution, driving the company's competitiveness and ensuring its relevance in the market.

Similarly, intangible assets enable businesses to adapt to changing market conditions and consumer preferences. Brands, trademarks, and goodwill help companies build strong relationships with customers, fostering loyalty and trust. These intangible assets play a key role in shaping the company's reputation and influencing consumer perception.

Intangible assets provide companies with a competitive edge, drive revenue growth, attract investors, and foster a culture of innovation. Businesses use them to position themselves for long-term success and sustainability.

The revenue potential of intangible assets is vast and often underestimated in traditional financial assessments. As businesses continue to innovate and invest in their intangible assets, they open up new avenues for generating revenue and expanding their market presence.

Intangible assets such as software, licenses, and contracts, provide a steady stream of income that contributes to the financial health of any company. For example, software companies often derive revenue from licensing fees or subscription models. This helps them to monetize their proprietary technology and innovative solutions. Moreover, businesses that hold valuable licenses or contracts can leverage these intangible assets to generate additional income through leasing or selling them.

CHAPTER FIVE

POLICIES AND PROCEDURES.

This may seem boring, but they are one of the back bones of every company, policies and procedures are very important, they can help clarify and reinforce the standards expected of the employee in all their professional dealings.

They also help employers manage staff effectively by defining what is acceptable and unacceptable within the Company/workplace.

These well-formed guidelines are also the backbone for HRM on the base of these policies and procedures they can form their directions and policies.

policies and procedures also provide a roadmap for the day-to-day operations. They ensure compliance with laws and regulations, give a guideline for decision-making, and streamline internal processes.

However, policies and procedures won't do your organization any good if your employees don't follow them, discipline is very important from both sides, as the CEO and managers create and enforce policies, it's important to make sure your staff understands why following policies and procedures is critical for their own benefit and safety.

When your employees follow policies and procedures, your business will use time and resources more efficiently. And this therefore enable you to grow and achieve your higher goals in no time.

Consistency in practices is also good for employees individually and safe work environment. They know what they're responsible for, how to work safely and what's expected of them, but also what they can expect from their supervisors and co-workers, Ongoing training is therefore most important.

Standard Operating Procedures, commonly referred to as SOPs, are important for businesses of all sizes.

Let's zoom in on why SOPs are so important, and how they impact on the daily functioning of your organization. A well-structured SOP should contain these essential sections that guide the reader through the process with ease:

Title Page: The title page of an SOP sets the foundation for the document, providing crucial information such as the SOP›s name, the date of creation or revision, and the department or team responsible for the process. This page serves as the first point of reference for anyone utilizing the SOP.

Preparatory Information: In this section, you›ll find an overview of the purpose and scope of the SOP. It may also include background information like regulatory requirements or industry standards that the process must adhere to. Preparatory information sets the stage for understanding the context in which the SOP operates.

Procedures Section: The heart of the SOP lies in the procedures section, where step-by-step instructions for executing the process are detailed. Each step should be clearly outlined, concise, and easy to follow. Consistency in style and format throughout this section is crucial for ensuring understanding and adherence to the SOP.

Quality Control and Assurance: To maintain the integrity and accuracy of the process, the quality control and assurance section outlines the necessary measures to be taken. This may include documentation requirements, record-keeping procedures, and verification processes to ensure that the desired outcome is consistently achieved.

WHAT ARE THE KEY CONSIDERATIONS WHEN WRITING AN SOP?

When writing a Standard Operating Procedure (SOP) for your company, keep these key considerations in mind to ensure its effectiveness and user-friendly usability.

Make sure you have the right format for your SOP. Make it a detailed document, the format should align with the nature of the processes within your business and the preferences (as much as possible) of all team members.

Involve all relevant stakeholders in the SOP development process because their input and expertise will ensure that the SOP reflects the collective and deeper knowledge and best practices of those directly involved in the process.

Before writing the SOP, clearly define the goals and objectives of the company and its process. This will help in aligning the SOP with desired outcomes and measuring its success effectively.

When creating your SOP, maintaining a consistent style, defining the structure and scope, and including all necessary steps are key to its clarity and effectiveness.

Testing the SOP in real-world scenarios before finalizing it is also necessary to ensure its accuracy and has practicality.

Always keep in mind to be flexible with all plans you create for your business as the real world is constantly on the move and subject to change.

BENEFITS OF STANDARD OPERATING PROCEDURES

The benefits of having Standard Operating Procedures (SOPs) in place for your business cannot be overstated. Here are most of the advantages that SOPs offers to organizations of all sizes or industries:

Consistency: SOPs promote consistency in how tasks are executed, ensuring that the same standards and procedures will be followed every time. This consistency minimizes errors, reduces variations in outcomes, and enhances overall efficiency within the organization.

Common Goals: With SOPs in place, teams can work towards the common goals more effectively. This because it aligns everyone on the same set of procedures, SOPs promote collaboration, coordination, and a sense of shared purpose among team members.

Communication: SOPs is a communication tool that provides clear guidelines for employees to follow. It outlines standardized processes and procedures to facilitate effective communication within teams and across departments and fosters a outline an understanding of how tasks should be performed.

Risk Management: SOPs outline procedures and protocols that must be followed in various situations, and that helps businesses to mitigate risks and therefore folds and ensure the safety of their employees and customers. For example, in industries such as healthcare and manufacturing, SOPs are used to ensure compliance with safety regulations and minimizing the risk of accidents or injuries. Therefore, they help to reduce potential liabilities and protect the company's reputation.

Training and Development: Businesses can ensure that their employees are properly trained and equipped to perform their roles effectively by providing new employees with detailed SOPs to follow. SOPs help new employees understand the expectations of their role, as well as the culture within the company and the standards and procedures that must be followed in order to be successful. This not only benefits the new employees, but also helps the business maintain a high level of productivity and efficiency.

Compliance with Industry Regulations: Businesses in highly regulated industries, such as Financials, pharmaceuticals, healthcare, and food services, rely on SOPs to ensure that they are meeting all legal requirements and industry standards. They help such businesses to demonstrate to regulators that they are operating in a compliant manner and reduce their risk of fines or penalties.

Uniformity in Procedures and Practices: SOPs also help ensure that all employees are on the same page and working towards the same goals as they provide employees clear, step-by-step instructions on how to complete their tasks. This consistency is needed for maintaining a high level of quality in products and services, as well as for avoiding errors and mistakes that can result from inconsistencies in procedures or expensive recalls and warranty claims.

Reminder and Reference: SOPs act as a valuable resource for employees, serving as a reminder of how tasks should be carried out. They provide a reference point for individuals to consult when faced with unfamiliar or complex processes, ensuring that they have clear guidance at their fingertips. It can also function as a benchmark for future training or HRM guidance on specific needs of employees.

HOW TO IMPLEMENT SOPS IN YOUR COMPANY?

Make an assessment of your current processes and identify areas that would benefit from a good SOP. Look for tasks that are repetitive or critical to your business, or sensitive to errors. Once you have pinpointed these processes, involve key stakeholders in the development of the SOPs to gain valuable insights.

Next you create a clear and detailed SOP plan that outlines the structure, format, and content requirements for each procedure. Just ensure that the instructions are easy to follow and understand, with a focus on clarity and precision. Assign responsibilities to individuals or teams for implementing and monitoring the SOPs and establish a timeline for completion. Training sessions may be necessary to familiarize employees with the SOPs and ensure proper implementation across the organization and repeat these trainings as well to secure it in the future.

As you roll out the SOPs, regularly monitor and evaluate their effectiveness in achieving the desired outcomes. Track performance metrics, gather feedback from users, and make adjustments as needed to improve efficiency and compliance (stay flexible at all times). Communication is key during the implementation phase, so keep all stakeholders informed of any updates or changes to the SOPs. Encourage a culture of continuous improvement by soliciting suggestions for enhancements and providing support to employees as they adapt to the new processes.

Lastly, integrate technology solutions to streamline SOP management, documentation, and training. Utilize software platforms that allow for easy access, version control, and tracking of SOPs, ensuring that the most up-to-date procedures are always available to employees. This will help you can enhance the efficiency and effectiveness of SOP implementation in your company.

Make it mandatory on your minutes of every board of directors' meetings.

MISTAKES TO AVOID WHEN CREATING SOPS

Mistakes will always be a part of us being human, as an aviation enthusiast and trainee pilot I am very well aware of policies and procedures before flying a plane you need to do your checks and every check list has his place in the whole of procedures before you can professionally and safely operate the flight.

This is why the SOP is so important within your business if you want to do things professional and do it the right way.

Neglecting Stakeholder Involvement: Simply by excluding key employees or departments, you risk overlooking valuable insights and expertise. It is necessary to gather input from those who will be directly impacted by the SOPs to ensure that the procedures are practical, efficient, and reflective of the actual workflow.

Overcomplicating the Procedures: Another pitfall to avoid is overcomplicating the SOPs with unnecessary details or convoluted steps. The goal of SOPs is to provide clear and straightforward instructions that can be easily followed by your employees. Keep the language simple, avoid technical jargon (when you can), and focus on the essential steps required to complete the task. Clarity is key when it comes to creating effective SOPs.

Lack of Regular Review and Updates: SOPs are not meant to be static documents. One mistake to avoid is failing to regularly review and update the procedures to reflect any changes in processes, technology, or regulations. Outdated SOPs can lead to confusion, errors, and non-compliance. Establish a schedule for reviewing and revising SOPs to ensure they remain accurate and relevant to the current operational environment, like all professionals keep themselves updated like doctors, lawyers, pilots and so on.

Failure to Provide Adequate Training: Implementing SOPs without proper training for employees is a common misstep that can hinder their effectiveness. Simply distributing the procedures without explaining their importance or providing hands-on training can result in confusion and resistance. Invest in comprehensive training programs to ensure that all employees understand the SOPs and feel confident in applying them to their daily tasks.

Ignoring Feedback and Continuous Improvement: a critical mistake to avoid is ignoring feedback from employees and overlooking opportunities for continuous improvement. SOPs should be seen as living documents that can be refined based on real-world experiences and feedback. Encourage open communication, gather suggestions for enhancements, and be willing to adapt the procedures to optimize their impact on operations. (look up KODAK)

Stay clear of these mistakes when creating SOPs if you desire to enhance their effectiveness and promote a culture of compliance and efficiency.

TRAINING YOUR EMPLOYEES ON SOPS

Training employees on Standard Operating Procedures (SOPs) is a necessary step in ensuring that these guidelines are effectively implemented and followed within your organization. Proper training equips your team with the knowledge and skills needed to adhere to the established processes, the HRM department will be the one to take all the necessary steps to make sure this all is coordinated and communicated to the responsible key personal within the business.

Here are some points to take in consideration when training your employees on SOPs:

Interactive Workshops: Conduct interactive workshops or training sessions to engage employees and facilitate hands-on learning. Encourage active participation and provide real-life examples to help employees understand the practical application of the SOPs.

Implementing quality system: Implementing a quality system as a guideline can also be helpful like *Total quality system* or *Kaizen (index).*

What Is Kaizen? Kaizen is a Japanese term meaning "change for the better" or as we say continuous improvement. It is a Japanese business philosophy that concerns the processes that continuously improve operations and involve all employees.

Kaizen sees improvement in productivity as a gradual and methodical process.

The concept of kaizen encompasses a wide range of ideas and areas. It involves making the work environment more efficient and effective by creating a team atmosphere, improving everyday procedures, ensuring employee engagement, and making a job more fulfilling, safer and less tiring.

These proven methods are absolutely worth considering implementing in your business, MAZDA has implemented KODO "soul of motion" it is also a

Japanese philosophy that has to do with arts performance and being excellent in what you create.

Role-Playing Exercises: Utilize role-playing exercises to simulate scenarios where employees must follow the SOPs. This hands-on approach allows staff to practice applying the procedures in a safe environment and reinforces their understanding of the processes.

Regular Assessments: Implement regular assessments or online questioners to evaluate employees' comprehension of the SOPs. This helps identify any gaps in knowledge and allows for targeted reinforcement of critical information.

Feedback Mechanism: Where employees can ask questions or provide input on the SOPs. Encouraging open communication fosters a culture of continuous improvement and ensures that the procedures remain relevant and effective.

Training employees on SOPs will enhance their individual performance. Investing in them should be seen as a plus to your business because well-trained employees are the cornerstone of a well-functioning organization.

UPDATING AND REVISING SOPS REGULARLY

As your company evolves and grows, you should regularly update and revise your Standard Operating Procedures (SOPs) to ensure they remain relevant and effective. This proactive approach helps maintain the integrity and efficiency of your processes. It also demonstrates a commitment to continuous improvement within your organization. Also keeping your quality systems in place and up to date to ensure your professionalism and overall quality.

If you solicit feedback from employees (middle management being the first to record these inputs) who work directly with the procedures, you can identify areas for enhancement and refinement. That collaborative approach will foster a culture of open communication and engagement. It will also ensure that your SOPs reflect the most efficient and effective ways of carrying out tasks.

Revising your SOPs on a regular basis (also on every management level within the business) helps you to incorporate lessons learned from past experiences and feedback because, when you analyse the outcomes of implemented procedures, you can easily identify areas of improvement and make necessary adjustments to optimize future performance.

In addition to staying compliant with industry standards and best practices, updating and revising your SOPs regularly can help mitigate risks and prevent costly errors. It will help you address any gaps or inconsistencies in your procedures, as well as reduce the likelihood of mistakes that could lead to operational disruptions or regulatory non-compliance. Proactive maintenance of your SOPs is a proactive strategy to safeguard your company›s reputation and financial well-being.

INTEGRATING TECHNOLOGY FOR SOP MANAGEMENT

As in today's digital age, technology plays a crucial role in streamlining your processes and increasing efficiency in your organization.

Integrating technology for the management of SOPs can greatly enhance their effectiveness. When you make use of software solutions and digital tools like a dashboard with integral ports to quickly navigate, you will have easy access to SOPs, streamline updates, and track compliance with regulatory requirements. It's a modern approach that saves time and improves the general workflow within an organization.

It also allows for centralized storage of all SOP documents. That means that your employees can easily access the most up-to-date versions. With cloud-based platforms and digital repositories, you can create a centralized hub for all SOPs. Such accessibility promotes consistency in task execution and reduces the risk of errors due to outdated information or misplaced documents.

Also, technology enables real-time updates and version control for SOPs. Technology ensures that any changes or revisions are instantly communicated to all relevant parties. With automated notifications and tracking features, companies can ensure that employees will always be working with the most current SOPs, thereby maintaining compliance with industry regulations and standards.

Incorporating technology into SOP management equally facilitates monitoring and reporting capabilities, allowing companies to track the usage and effectiveness of their SOPs. Through analytics and data insights, organizations can identify areas for improvement, measure the impact of SOPs on performance metrics, and make data-driven decisions to optimize processes.

With the right strategies in place, SOPs can truly transform the way your company operates and help you achieve your desired goals and beyond with precision.

INDEPENDENT CORPORATE STRUCTURE (NOT ON ONE PERSON-BASED MODEL)

This is a key item to plan very carefully as it means what will happen to the company when key figures leave the company or even die, will the company still be able to survive and continue operation.

For example, companies like Procter and gamble, system banks, food manufacturers and medicine manufacturers are so important to society and the world they need to be reliable and continues to secure our supply chain.

So, the importance to established standards and frameworks must not be overlooked when considering continuity in business, these guiding principles will offer a structured approach to identifying risks, formulating strategies, and implementing measures to bolster preparedness.

When your company has to comply with renowned standards such as ISO 22301:2019 and the Business Continuity Institute's Good Practice Guidelines, your company will be able to easily manage disruptions with a strategic roadmap in hand. The frameworks emphasize a realistic perspective on business continuity. They should include technical solutions, governance protocols, communication strategies, and comprehensive training initiatives. Also, standards such as the National Institute of Standards and Technology's (NIST) Framework for Improving Critical Infrastructure Cybersecurity can offer invaluable insights into mitigating cyber risks and fortifying digital resilience.

Business continuity is not just a set of protocols or plans; it is a mindset ingrained in the corporate structure of a business. The role of leadership, governance, and cross-functional collaboration help to guarantee the success of business continuity efforts. An organization that prioritizes business continuity as an integral part of its corporate structure will be able to safeguard its operations and emerge stronger in the long run.

The business continuity plan will also be a must when the business is a part of a family office structure, these multiple owning family offices need solid structures to be able to continue and secure the intergenerational wealth.

And this also applies for recipes (for medicines or cola and more) and data on science when dealing with a knowledge / engineering or other type of important companies.

BUSINESS MODEL THAT SECURES AND MAKES MONEY.

Making money is a necessity for a commercial and for-profit operating company, words as Cash-flow and turnover will pass every time but the real secret lies in the SYSTEM not in money itself.

That system is a business model, there are a lot of variants, but they don't always benefit your kind of company or the activities your company is involved in.

Why the Business Models Matter? we have to go back to the first principles of your company to make a simple and useful distinction, pointing out that a business model is a description of how your business runs and intents to make a profit, but a competitive strategy only explains how you will be better than your competitors.

These business models also help investors evaluate companies and this makes your company more professional and investible.

One of the biggest mistakes many companies make when they create their business models is to underestimate the costs of funding the business until it becomes profitable. Counting the costs until the introduction of a product is not good enough. The company has to keep the business running until its revenues exceed their expenses.

A business model is really a set of assumptions or hypotheses one of many models is the business model canvas it is essentially an organized way to lay out your assumptions about not only your key resources and your key activities of your value chain, but also your value proposition, customer relationships, customers, channels, cost structures, and revenue streams, it's important to compare your model with others, and see if you are competitive enough.

Developing a business model is a unique approach to gaining a sustainable advantage over your rivals. It involves making deliberate choices about how you will compete in the market, differentiate your offerings, and position your brand against competitors.

But what business models are there to choose from?

There are various types of business models that companies can adopt:

SUBSCRIPTION MODEL: With this business model, your customers pay a recurring fee for access to your product or service. This model is popular in industries such as media, software, and telecommunications, where customers value ongoing access to content or services.

Companies like Netflix and Spotify have thrived by offering subscription-based services to their customers. If you are in such industries, this may be the perfect business model to adopt.

E-commerce Model: The e-commerce business model is often adopted by companies which sell products or services online through a website or mobile app. This model has gained popularity in recent years due to the rise of digital technology and changing consumer preferences. Alibaba, for example, has used this business model to revolutionize the way we shop by offering a wide range of products online.

Freemium Model: This business model enables a company to offer a basic version of their product or service for free, with the option to upgrade to a premium version for additional features or functionality. It is used by software companies like Evernote to attract users and drive revenue through premium subscriptions.

On-demand Model: This is a business model that has become increasingly popular in the transportation and food delivery industries. Companies like Uber and printing on demand have disrupted traditional business models by offering on-demand services that provide customers with convenience and flexibility.

But any company that will adopt this model should be aware that it relies on technology to connect customers with service providers in real-time.

Franchise Business Model: Franchisees pay an upfront fee and ongoing royalties to operate a business under an established brand name and business model. Companies like McDonald's and Subway have successfully used the franchise model to grow their businesses globally. The model is popular among companies that want to expand their brand and reach a wider market without having to establish new locations themselves.

Platform Business Model: Platform business model is a digital-based model that help companies to create value by connecting two or more groups of users and facilitating transactions between them. You can see this with Airbnb, which has created successful platforms by matching supply with demand.

The Razor and Blade Model: It is a business model where companies sell a primary product at a low cost or even for free but make a profit from selling complementary products or services. Gillette, for example, uses this model by selling razors or coffee machines at a low cost, but make a profit from selling razor blades or coffee pods.

Direct Sales Business Model: This business model is commonly used by companies that sell products or services directly to consumers through a network of independent sales representatives. Avon used this model to build successful businesses. The model helped it leverage the personal relationships and sales skills of their representatives and, as a result, drive sales.

Asset-Light Business Model: With this type of business model, a company can outsource non-core functions to third-party providers to reduce costs and focus on their core competencies. A good example is Nike.

Understand that business models and company's strategies must align with a string of things that make up your business and make it unique. So, follow the below when considering what business model to choose:

CRAFTING YOUR COMPETITIVE EDGE

To develop a strong business model, you must first identify what sets your company apart from the competition. What unique value do you offer to customers that others cannot replicate?

When you clearly understand your strengths, weaknesses, opportunities, and threats, you can pinpoint areas where you can excel and outperform your rivals. That will also determine the business model you can adopt. Your competitive edge could stem from superior product quality, exceptional customer service, innovative technology, or efficient operations. Once you've identified your competitive edge, you can choose a business model and build your strategy around leveraging this advantage to capture market share and drive profitability.

STANDING OUT IN THE MARKET

Your business model should focus on how you will differentiate your brand and offerings to appeal to your target audience. This could involve creating a unique brand identity, offering customized solutions, or providing a superior customer experience. Strive to clearly define what sets you apart from your competitors so that you can carve out a distinct position in the market and attract customers who value what you have to offer.

ADAPTING TO MARKET DYNAMICS

Every industry today constantly evolves, with new trends, technologies, and competitors emerging all the time. To stay competitive, ensure that the business model you choose is flexible and adaptable to changes in the market. But make sure you continuously monitor market dynamics, customer preferences, and competitor actions to identify opportunities and threats, and review your business strategies accordingly.

WHY YOU SHOULD ALIGN BUSINESS MODELS AND COMPETITIVE STRATEGIES

You have to align your business model with your competitive strategy to drive the profitability and long-term success of your company. These two components work hand in hand to establish a solid foundation for your business and differentiate you from competitors.

To align your business model and competitive strategy effectively, consider the below factors:

Understanding Your Value Proposition: Your business model should clearly define how you create and deliver value to customers, while your competitive strategy should outline how you differentiate your offerings from competitors.

Identifying Customer Relationships: Your business model should specify how you engage with customers, while your competitive strategy should focus on attracting and retaining customers in a competitive market.

Streamlining Cost Structures: Your business model should optimize cost structures to support your value proposition, while your competitive strategy should ensure that your costs are competitive in the market.

HOW TO DRIVE PROFITABILITY THROUGH YOUR BUSINESS MODEL

Once you understand your target market, revenue streams, and cost structure, you can ensure that your financials align for a profitable venture. It allows you to identify market opportunities and develop products or services that meet the needs of your customers effectively.

To drive profitability through your business model, focus on delivering value to your target market. As simple as this may sound, it can help you generate higher profits. One key aspect of driving profitability through your business model is continuously evaluating and refining your assumptions and strategies. A smart investor constantly compares their business model with others in the industry to identify areas where they can improve and stay ahead of the competition.

HOW TO LEVERAGE COMPETITIVE ADVANTAGE

Understanding what sets your company apart from others in the market can effectively position you for long-term profitability and growth.

Here are some strategies to help you leverage your competitive advantage for success:

IDENTIFY YOUR STRENGTHS

Take stock of what makes your company special and differentiates you from competitors.

FOCUS ON CUSTOMER VALUE

Your competitive advantage should benefit your customers. Ensure you deliver value to your target audience in a way that your competitors can't replicate. That will help build customer loyalty and drive profitability.

STAY AHEAD OF TRENDS

Keep a pulse on industry trends and consumer preferences to anticipate changes in the market. You have to be proactive and adapt to new developments so that you can maintain your competitive edge.

CONTINUOUS IMPROVEMENT

Don't rest on your laurels. Continuously seek ways to enhance your products, services, and operations to stay ahead of the competition. Therefore, embrace innovation and strive for excellence in all aspects of your business.

TURBOCHARGING THE CORE BUSINESS FOR PROFITABILITY

You want to achieve profitability Then turbocharge your core business line. You should deepen and expand your existing capabilities as it will capture more value from your core operations.

This allows you to leverage your strengths and differentiate yourself in the market. As you focus on what your company does best, you will be able to maximize the potential of your core business and set yourself up for sustainable growth and success.

This strategy not only boosts profitability but also reinforces your company's reputation as a leader in your industry. But it requires investing in research, development, and technology to enhance your products or services.

CONCLUSION

There are various types of business models that companies can adopt based on their industry, target market, and competition. Understanding these different models is needed for businesses to stay competitive and profitable in any business environment. If you choose the right business model and continually adapt to changing market conditions, your business will enjoy long-term success and sustainable growth.

THE COST- VOLUME-PROFIT MODEL (CVP)

The operating profit can also be overlooked capital within the company, CVP has more than one way to be viewed the most common one is the Breakeven point. The breakeven point is the number of units that need to be sold or the amount of sales revenue that must be generated in order to cover your costs required to make the product.

To calculate this Breakeven point the most basic calculation that can be used is:

$$\text{Breakeven Sales Volume} = CMFC$$
$$FC = \text{Fixed costs } CM = \text{Contribution}$$
$$\text{margin} = \text{Sales} - \text{Variable Costs}$$

THE BOARD OF DIRECTORS AND THEIR RESPONSIBILITIES.

There is a set of people who make up the top of a company the bigger the company the more complex (and layers) there will be, and the board of directors has one of the most important roles as it facilitates (or hire) the CEO and therefore the day-to-day operations general manager.

More responsibilities are:

1. Recruit the CEO , Supervise and evaluate the general manager.
2. create and maintain policies and procedures and governance systems.

3. Give direction for the organisation.
4. Keep oversite and govern the relationship with the CEO and govern the organisation.
5. The duty to protect assets of the company and the stakeholders /shareholders investments.
6. Control function and monitoring.

Let's look at what exactly this esteemed group does. How do they carry out the responsibilities that come with overseeing a company's operations? We will equally discuss how they handle the strategic planning, risk management, and ethical standards that shape a company's path forward.

TYPES OF A COMPANY'S BOARD

There are various types of boards based on their composition, structure, and function. The most common types of company boards include executive, non-executive, independent, and advisory boards.

EXECUTIVE BOARD

Executive board is composed of individuals who are also part of the management team of the company. These individuals hold executive positions such as CEO, CFO, COO, etc. They are responsible for making operational decisions and implementing strategies on a day-to-day basis.

NON-EXECUTIVE BOARD

Non-executive board comprises of individuals who are not part of the company's management team. They provide an external perspective and offer guidance and oversight to the executive team. Non-executive directors bring a diverse set of skills and experience to the board, helping to ensure good governance and sound decision-making.

INDEPENDENT BOARD

Independent board comprises of individuals who are not affiliated with the company in any way. They are considered impartial and free from any conflicts of interest. Independent directors are often needed for providing unbiased advice and oversight, especially in cases where there are conflicts of interest among other board members.

ADVISORY BOARD

Advisory board is another type of board that is typically composed of external experts and industry professionals who offer strategic advice and guidance to the company. Advisory boards do not have any formal decision-making powers but provide valuable insights and recommendations to help the company succeed. They often focus on specific areas such as marketing, technology, or finance.

JOINT BOARD

This is made up of both internal executives and external directors. This type of board is common in large corporations where executives work closely with outside directors to make strategic decisions and provide oversight. Joint boards help to bridge the gap between management and external viewpoints. The aim is to ensure a balanced approach to governance.

Meanwhile, some companies also have rotating boards, where directors serve for a limited term before rotating out and being replaced by new members. This type of board structure helps to bring in fresh perspectives and diverse expertise on a regular basis, ensuring continuity and innovation within the company.

Also, there are boards with special committees focused on specific areas such as audit, compensation, and governance.

These committees are composed of a subset of board members who have expertise in these areas and provide detailed recommendations and oversight on key issues. Special committees help to ensure that the board is addressing critical issues effectively.

FUNCTIONS OF A COMPANY'S BOARD OF DIRECTORS

The board of directors plays a pivotal role in charting the company's course toward long-term goals and objectives. They collaborate with senior management to set the strategic direction, evaluate market conditions, and identify growth opportunities. Their collaborative effort ensures that the company remains focused on maximizing shareholder value and achieving sustainable growth.

The following are their functions in any organization:

- Representation of Independent and Diverse Perspectives
- The eclectic mix of backgrounds, expertise, and experiences inherent in a board, ensures that the board can offer a wide array of insights and challenge conventional thinking.

A board is powerful because of the following reasons:

- The board members are carefully selected to be independent, free from conflicts of interest, and capable of acting in the best interests of the company and its stakeholders.
- This diversity of perspectives not only enhances the board's decision-making process but also fosters a culture of inclusivity and creativity within the company.
- By representing a broad spectrum of viewpoints, the board can effectively handle complex issues, anticipate challenges, and drive innovation in the company's strategic direction.

As the board of directors' grapples with the intricacies of corporate governance, the ability to ask tough and probing questions becomes paramount. Through critical examination of the company's operations, financial performance, and strategic initiatives, board members can hold management accountable and ensure transparency.

ASKING TOUGH AND PROBING QUESTIONS

The board of directors must not shy away from asking tough and probing questions. This aspect of their role involves delving deep into the company's operations, financial performance, and strategic initiatives. They challenge assumptions and seek clarification. This questioning process not only enhances the board's understanding of the company's inner workings but also holds management accountable for their decisions and actions.

To maintain transparency and accountability within the company, the board must actively engage in asking tough and probing questions during board meetings and discussions. It must encourage open dialogue and debate so that it can uncover potential blind spots, gaps in information, or conflicting priorities that need to be addressed.

The art of asking tough and probing questions requires a delicate balance of assertiveness, curiosity, and empathy from board members. They must be assertive in seeking clarity and accountability, curious in exploring different perspectives and possibilities, and empathetic in understanding the implications of their inquiries on others. This is why very experienced persons often constitute a company's board.

WELL-INFORMED AND FULLY ENGAGED WITH MAJOR ISSUES

If you want your company to stand the test of time, don't elect passive board members - board members must stay well-informed and fully engaged with major issues facing the company. This level of involvement requires a commitment to continuous learning and a keen awareness of industry trends. Being fully engaged entails attending board meetings, reviewing relevant materials, and seeking input from key stakeholders.

Board members are tasked with not only understanding the major issues facing the company but also with providing guidance on how to address these challenges.

Their informed perspective and engagement are going to be needed in shaping the company's strategic direction and long-term goals.

So, they have to stay abreast of industry developments and market conditions. When you have a table of lazy board members, your company will crash anytime soon.

Board members must be vigilant in their pursuit of knowledge and engagement with major issues. That is their primary role in any company. Their dedication to staying informed and fully engaged is important in steering the company toward success and sustainability.

HOW YOU AS OWNER CAN GET FIRED FROM YOUR OWN COMPANY.

Yes, you can get fired from your own company, but firstly you need to have a function within the company if you are only a share/stakeholder it does not apply to you.

So 'have you ever considered the possibility of being fired from your own company? As a company owner, the idea may seem far-fetched, but it is necessary to understand the risks that come with your position. One such risk is termination by the board of directors in corporations. This scenario can unfold if the board deems your continued presence detrimental to the company's success. That sounds unbelievable, right? But, in business, it is possible that a company owner may face the unthinkable - being dismissed from their own creation.

Operating Agreement Flexibility: In Limited Liability Companies (LLCs or LTD's and so on), the operating agreement holds significant importance in determining the potential consequences for the owner. This agreement serves as a guiding document that outlines conditions under which members, including the company owner, can be removed from their management roles or even expelled from the company entirely. The agreement allows for a tailored approach to addressing conflicts or misconduct within the business structure.

While specific examples of LLC / LTD (and so on) owners being fired from their own companies were not provided in the information, the potential consequences outlined in the operating agreement can vary based on the circumstances. Instances of severe misconduct, breaches of fiduciary duties, or repeated conflicts within the management team could trigger clauses for the removal of the owner. Understanding the implications of these scenarios is very important for owners to mitigate risks and maintain a harmonious business environment.

Now, let's go into a number of key issues that will help understand the subject matter.

EXPLORING PROVISIONS IN CORPORATION BYLAWS FOR REMOVING OFFICERS OR DIRECTORS

In corporations, the bylaws play a vital role in outlining the procedures and criteria for removing officers or directors, including the company owner. This internal regulation serves as a safeguard for the company and its shareholders. They ensure that individuals in positions of authority can be removed if their actions are detrimental to the company's interests. Through the incorporation of such provisions in the bylaws, the company establishes a clear framework for addressing issues of misconduct or incompetence that may arise in the future.

When it comes to the removal of officers or directors, including the company owner, the bylaws must adhere to legal requirements and principles of fairness. These provisions offer a structured approach to dealing with situations where individuals fail to fulfil their duties or act in a manner that jeopardizes the company's well-being.

To protect the owner's position and ensure transparency in governance, corporations must establish clear and comprehensive bylaws. These provisions should detail the process for removing officers or directors, lay out the criteria for such actions, and establish a fair and objective mechanism for decision-making.

RECOGNIZING THE LEGAL ACTION SHAREHOLDERS CAN TAKE

Business owners must recognize the power shareholders hold and the actions they can take in response to misconduct. In situations involving legal or ethical misconduct by the majority owner, shareholders have the right to take legal action to address the issue.

OWNERS MUST BEAR THESE IN MIND

A legal action can be initiated if the majority owner breaches their fiduciary duties or engages in unlawful activities that jeopardize the company's reputation and financial well-being. Shareholders play a crucial role in ensuring accountability and transparency within the organization.

Examples of misconduct that may lead to legal action include embezzlement, or other serious ethical violations. If shareholders gather enough evidence to substantiate their claims, they can pursue legal avenues to remove the majority owner from their position.

Shareholders have to act in the best interests of the company and its stakeholders. They have to hold the majority owner accountable for their actions because they must uphold ethical standards and maintain the company's integrity.

I cannot emphasize enough to go to a legal expert to look over your specific case as this is so important. (this book only provides you with insight into these situations and cannot be seen as legal or any other advice)

STRATEGIES FOR PROTECTING YOUR POSITION AS THE OWNER

As the owner of your company, you need to implement strategic measures to safeguard your position and mitigate the risk of being fired.

Before going into details, here are ways how you can achieve this:

1. CLEAR AGREEMENTS

One effective strategy is to draft clear and comprehensive agreements, such as operating agreements in the case of LLCs/LTDs, that explicitly outline the rights and responsibilities of each member. You need to clearly define the conditions under which members can be removed. With that, you'll be able to establish a transparent and fair process that protects your interests. It will also help in maintaining control and stability within the company.

2. ETHICAL OPERATIONS

Operating ethically, complying with legal requirements, and managing the company's finances effectively can significantly reduce the likelihood of facing allegations of legal or ethical misconduct. Make sure that you uphold high standards of professionalism and integrity so that you can protect your reputation and build trust with stakeholders.

3. STAKEHOLDERS INVOLVEMENT

Foster open lines of communication, showcase your leadership capabilities, and involve stakeholders in decision-making processes. That will help cultivate trust and support from those who hold influence within the company. Nurturing these relationships can be instrumental in garnering backing during challenging times and solidifying your role as the leader of the organization.

4. INVOLVEMENT OF LEGAL EXPERTS

Seeking legal advice is a proactive step that all owners should consider safeguarding their position and control conflicts effectively. Legal professionals can offer guidance on pertinent laws and regulations, assist in drafting agreements, and ensure that your rights and obligations are protected. Engaging legal counsel can provide you with the expertise and resources needed to address any legal challenges or disputes that may arise.

It can also be very smart to have your own inhouse lawyer (full time or part time) this saves a lot of time and money.

I cannot emphasize enough to go to a legal expert to look over your specific case as this is so important. (this book only provides you with insight into these situations and cannot be seen as legal or any other advice)

DRAFTING CLEAR AGREEMENTS TO SAFEGUARD YOUR RIGHTS

These agreements, such as operating agreements in the case of Limited liability company's (or entities), serve as the foundation for outlining the rights and responsibilities of each member involved. When you clearly outline the procedures for removal and the criteria that must be met, you can create a sense of clarity and accountability within the organization. This not only protects your rights as the owner but also promotes a culture of fairness and respect among all stakeholders of your company.

Having well-defined agreements in place can provide you with leverage in case of disputes or disagreements. If the situation arises where your position as the owner is challenged, a carefully drafted operating agreement can serve as evidence of the agreed-upon terms and conditions. This can help you defend your rights and make a compelling case for maintaining your role within the company.

MAINTAINING GOOD BUSINESS PRACTICES TO MINIMIZE RISKS

By following ethical guidelines and staying compliant with legal requirements, you can minimize the risks of facing allegations of misconduct.

To ensure the longevity of your role, consider the following strategies:

- Operate ethically: Uphold high moral standards in all business dealings to build trust with stakeholders.
- Stay compliant: Adhere to legal regulations and requirements to avoid any legal issues that could jeopardize your position.
- Manage finances effectively: Implement sound financial practices to ensure the company's stability and growth.

You just have to observe each of the above because prevention is key in safeguarding against unforeseen challenges that could threaten your ownership.

BUILDING STRONG RELATIONSHIPS WITH STAKEHOLDERS

Engaging with stakeholders on a regular basis allows you to gather valuable insights and feedback that can help shape the direction of the company. Listen to their concerns and ideas to show that you value their input and are dedicated to making informed decisions that benefit all parties involved. It will strengthen the bond between you and your stakeholders.

You have to lead by example to instil trust and respect in those around you. Effective communication, delegation, and conflict-resolution skills are components of effective leadership that can help you address challenges and build lasting partnerships with stakeholders.

Involving stakeholders in the decision-making process can also lead to greater buy-in and support for company initiatives. By soliciting feedback, sharing information, and seeking input from stakeholders, you create a sense of ownership and involvement that can drive engagement and enthusiasm for the company's goals.

SEEKING LEGAL ADVICE FOR PROTECTION AND GUIDANCE

When faced with the unsettling prospect of being fired from your own creation, seeking legal advice is not just a prudent step but a major one. Legal professionals possess the expertise and knowledge needed to protect your rights and provide guidance on the intricacies of relevant laws and regulations.

Legal advice can offer a layer of protection against potential threats to your ownership position, whether they stem from internal conflicts or external challenges. With the guidance of legal professionals, you can manage the complexities of company ownership with confidence and clarity.

Being fired from your own company is a distressing possibility that every owner should be aware of. Understanding the risks associated with termination by the board of directors or legal actions from shareholders is a must. You have to know the provisions in your company's bylaws and have clear agreements in place to protect your position as the owner. You also have to consider maintaining good business practices, building strong relationships with stakeholders, and seeking legal advice when needed.

CHAPTER SIX

DEFINE CAPITAL.

To put it in simple terms, capital refers to the financial assets and resources that are used to generate income or wealth. Capital is essential for your business to function and grow. It can take many forms, including, equipment, inventory, cash, investments, and property. It can also be seen as the money or wealth used to operate a business. This includes the funds needed to start the business, as well as the ongoing resources necessary for day-to-day operations. For example, a company may need capital to pay employees, and cover other expenses. Without sufficient capital, a business may struggle to survive or expand.

Understanding the different forms of capital and how they interconnect is necessary for business owners and investors to make informed decisions and drive their organizations towards success.

Capital can be one of these hidden assets within your business to define this is very important.

To give you an impression of the types of capital:

- Physical (real asset) / Working Capital / Fixed Capital / Financial Capital
- Human Capital / Equity Capital / Loan Capital / Intellectual Capital
- Social Capital / Information Capital / Natural Capital and
- Fictitious Capital are just a few in a row of meany.

I will define a few forms of capital in depth:

PHYSICAL CAPITAL

Physical capital refers to the tangible assets that a business uses to produce goods or services, such as buildings, vehicles, and other important equipment. These assets are needed for the functioning of a business and help to determine its productivity and profitability. Effective management of physical capital is therefore essential for your business to succeed and thrive.

A major concept related to physical capital management is the idea of investment. Businesses must invest in physical capital in order to acquire the necessary assets for them to operate and grow their operations and /or expansions. This investment can take the form of purchasing new machinery, upgrading existing equipment, or expanding facilities to accommodate growth.

Smart investments in physical capital can increase a business' efficiency and output. The outcome will be increased revenues and profitability in the long run.

Just like any asset, physical capital also requires regular maintenance to ensure that it functions properly and remains in good condition. Neglecting maintenance can lead to breakdowns, downtime, and reduced productivity, all of which can have a negative impact on a business's bottom line.

Physical capital management also involves the optimization of assets. Businesses needs to ensure that their physical capital is utilized in the most efficient and effective manner possible to maximize returns. This can involve proper scheduling of equipment usage, minimizing downtime, and identifying opportunities for consolidation or outsourcing to reduce costs.

As a professional business you must be aware of the risks associated with these physical assets, such as equipment failure, accidents, or obsolescence, and take steps to mitigate these risks. The business needs to implement safety protocols, acquiring insurance coverage, or developing contingency plans to address potential threats to physical capital.

As technology continues to evolve at a rapid pace, businessowners/ CEO's must stay abreast of new developments and opportunities to enhance their physical capital. They may have to adopt new technologies, such as automation or robotics, to improve productivity and efficiency, or implement digital tools to track and monitor the performance of physical assets.

WORKING CAPITAL

Working capital refers to the amount of money a company has available to cover its day-to-day operations. Essentially, working capital is the difference between a company's current assets and current liabilities. Your current assets include accounts receivable, inventory, and other assets that can be easily converted into cash within a year, while your current liabilities consist of debts and obligations that are due within a year.

The purpose of working capital is to ensure that a company can meet its short-term financial obligations, including payment for day-to-day expenses such as rent, utilities, wages, and supplier bills. Without sufficient working capital, a business may struggle to meet these obligations. That will result in cash flow problems and potentially even insolvency / bankruptcy.

Another important aspect of working capital management is to ensure that a company has enough liquidity to seize any opportunities that may arise. For example, having sufficient working capital can allow a business to take advantage of discounts offered by suppliers for early payment, or to invest in new equipment or technology that can improve efficiency and productivity.

Proper management of working capital involves striking the right balance between maintaining enough cash to cover short-term obligations and avoiding excessive idle cash that could be put to better use elsewhere. This requires careful monitoring of cash flow, inventory levels, accounts receivable, and accounts payable to ensure that the company's working capital is being used effectively and efficiently.

There are several key components that make up working capital: accounts receivable, inventory, cash and accounts payable.

Cash is the most liquid form of working capital and is used to cover immediate expenses. Accounts receivable represents money owed to the company by customers for goods or services rendered. Inventory includes goods that are ready for sale and represents an investment that tied up in the business. Accounts payable are obligations that the company owes to suppliers and other creditors.

The efficient management of working capital can help a company to reduce its reliance on external financing, improve cash flow, and increase profitability and over sustainable periods of time it will also build up wealth withing your company.

FIXED CAPITAL

Key to the concept of fixed capital is its contrast with circulating capital, emphasizing the durable nature of assets that are pivotal for business operations. While circulating capital includes raw materials and day-to-day expenses, fixed capital comprises long-lasting investments that underpin the core functions of a company. It refers to the long-term assets that a company owns and uses to produce goods or services. These assets are not easily converted into cash and are essential for the operation of the business. Understanding the concepts of fixed capital is helpful for business owners and managers to make informed decisions regarding investments, budgeting, and growth strategies.

Physical assets such as buildings, machinery, equipment, and vehicles are primary components of fixed capital. These assets are necessary for the production process and are often costly to acquire. For example, a manufacturing company may need specialized machinery to produce goods efficiently, while a transportation company may require a fleet of vehicles to deliver products to customers.

Investing in high-quality physical assets can improve productivity and competitiveness in the market.

Another important aspect of fixed capital is technological assets, such as software, patents, and intellectual property. These assets are important for staying ahead of competitors and adapting to changes in the industry. A software company may invest in developing proprietary software to offer unique features to customers, while a pharmaceutical company may patent a new drug to protect its intellectual property rights.

Fixed capital also includes intangible assets like brand reputation, customer relationships, and goodwill. These assets are valuable but difficult to quantify on the balance sheet. For example, a well-established brand can command higher prices and customer loyalty, while strong relationships with suppliers can lead to better terms and discounts. Building and maintaining intangible assets require time, effort, and resources, but they can contribute significantly to the overall value of the business.

Business owners and managers need to evaluate the performance of assets regularly and make strategic decisions based on the financial data. For example, if a company's machinery is outdated and inefficient, it may be more cost-effective to replace it with newer equipment rather than continue repairs and maintenance.

Similarly, if a company's intellectual property is underutilized, it may be beneficial to license it to other businesses or explore new revenue streams.

Investing in fixed capital requires care full planning and analysis to ensure a positive return on investment. Companies need to consider various factors such as the expected lifespan of assets, depreciation rates, maintenance costs, and technological obsolescence. A company, for instance, may choose to lease equipment instead of buying it outright to avoid tying up capital and risk exposure to market fluctuations. Companies may also consider outsourcing certain functions to reduce overhead costs and focus on core competencies.

In conclusion, the concepts of fixed capital in business are essential for creating value, generating profits, and sustaining competitive advantage. Always ensure the continuous evaluation and optimization of fixed capital investments, as that is critical for adapting to changing market conditions and achieving sustainable growth.

FINANCIAL CAPITAL

When it comes to exploring financial capital options for your business, here are some key considerations to keep in mind as you navigate the realm of financial capital:

Debt vs. Equity: One of the fundamental choices you will encounter is whether to raise capital through debt or equity financing. Debt financing involves borrowing money that must be repaid with interest, while equity financing involves selling ownership stakes in your company. Each option has its upside or downside, so it's important to carefully weigh the implications for your business's financial health and long-term growth.

Sources of Financial Capital: Financial capital can be sourced from various types of avenues, including traditional banks, venture capital firms, angel investors, and crowdfunding platforms. Each source comes with its own set of requirements and terms and conditions, so you need to explore multiple options to find the best fit for your business's needs. When you diversify your sources of financial capital, you reduce risk and increase your chances of securing the funding you need.

Strategic Use of Financial Capital: How you deploy your financial capital can significantly impact your business's success. Whether you're looking to expand operations, launch a new product, or invest in marketing initiatives, have a clear strategy in place. This is because aligning your financial capital with your business goals and objectives, helps you maximize the return on investment and set your company up for sustainable growth.

Risk Management: Financial capital comes with inherent risks, and you have to manage these risks effectively to safeguard your business's financial stability. Things like market fluctuations and unexpected expenses can affect your financial capital.

HUMAN CAPITAL

Human capital is a term used in business to refer to the skills, knowledge, and experience possessed by employees that are essential to the success of a company. It encompasses the idea that people are the most important asset a business has. Therefore, managing this asset effectively is vital for achieving organizational goals and maintaining a competitive advantage in the marketplace.

Employees are not just a cost to be minimized, but an investment to be maximized. This means that to maximise your investment in this asset it is wise to invest in your employees through training, development, and support in order to unlock their full potential and drive business success.

Effective management of human capital often involves recognizing and rewarding employees for their contributions to the organization. This can be done through performance evaluations, promotions, bonuses, and other forms of recognition that demonstrate the value the company places on its employees.

When you establish a culture of appreciation and support, your business can foster loyalty and commitment among the workforces. You will be able to build a strong team of professionals who are dedicated to achieving your company's goals.

Try to embrace diversity and inclusion. It will help your company tap into a wider pool of talent, foster creativity and innovation, and improve its decision-making processes. Research has shown that diverse teams are more productive and innovative, as they bring a variety of viewpoints and ideas to the table, leading to better outcomes for the business.

In addition, managing human capital also requires effective communication and collaboration within the organization. Clear communication channels, regular feedback, and open dialogue between employees and managers are bring everyone on the same page, so that they work towards a common goal. Collaboration and teamwork are important for driving innovation and problem-solving, as different perspectives can lead to more creative solutions to challenges that arise in the business.

To effectively manage your human capital, consider offering flexible work arrangements, providing opportunities for work-life balance, and fostering a culture of respect and support among your workers. Research has shown that happy and engaged employees are more productive, creative, and loyal to their organization.

Construct your company culture around the desire to attract top talent by offering competitive benefits, salaries and opportunities for growth, while also retaining your best employees by providing a positive work environment, opportunities for advancement, and recognition for their contributions. If you build a strong employer brand and reputation, your business will be able to attract and retain the best talent in the industry. That gives you a competitive edge in the marketplace.

INTELLECTUAL CAPITAL

Intellectual capital, often referred to as the knowledge and expertise within an organization, is an asset that drives innovation and growth. Harnessing this capital involves recognizing and utilizing the unique skills and insights of employees to generate new ideas and solutions.

Investing in the development of intellectual capital through training programs, mentorship initiatives, and continuous learning opportunities can enhance the innovative capacity of a company. Meanwhile, recognizing and rewarding employees for their innovative contributions can also motivate them to actively participate in the innovation process and contribute to the company's success.

Intellectual capital is not limited to individual expertise but also includes the collective intelligence and institutional knowledge that exist within your organization (like special recipes or ingredients mix for medicines). Companies that effectively leverage the intellectual resources at their disposal can adapt to changing market conditions, anticipate industry trends, and stay ahead of competitors.

SOCIAL CAPITAL

When you invest time and effort in cultivating relationships with others, you are not only building a network but also creating valuable opportunities for collaboration and growth. Social capital goes beyond mere connections; it is about establishing trust, reciprocity, and support within your professional community. If you actively engage with others, you can access resources, knowledge, and opportunities that can propel your business forward.

Attending industry events, conferences, and networking gatherings, for instance, allows you to meet new people and expand your circle of contacts. These interactions provide a platform for sharing ideas, exchanging insights, and forming mutually beneficial partnerships. Building social capital through networking is an ongoing process that requires genuine engagement and a willingness to connect with others on a meaningful level.

Today, social media platforms can be very useful in building social capital. Platforms like LinkedIn, Twitter, and Facebook offer opportunities to connect with industry professionals, share knowledge, and showcase your expertise. Participating in online discussions, sharing relevant content, and engaging with your peers, can enhance your visibility and credibility within your industry.

Building social capital is not just about expanding your network; it is also about giving back and supporting others in your community. And remember that social capital is a two-way street; the more you invest in nurturing your connections, the greater the returns you will see in terms of opportunities, insights, and growth for your business.

OTHER FORMS OF CAPITAL

The definitions of fictitious, informational, and natural capitals highlight the diverse forms of wealth and resources that contribute to the well-being of business and the society, at large. Each type of capital has its own characteristics and implications for economic development and sustainability. Fictitious capital plays an important role in financial markets, informational capital drives innovation and productivity, and natural capital sustains ecosystems and biodiversity. Having an understanding the interplay and dynamics of these different forms of capital will help you develop quality policies and strategies that promote inclusive and sustainable growth in your business.

FICTITIOUS CAPITAL

This is also known as financial capital. It refers to assets that do not have any physical or tangible form but represent claims on real wealth. Examples of fictitious capital include stocks, bonds, and derivatives. While these assets may not have inherent value on their own, they help in the proper functioning of financial markets and the allocation of resources within an economy. Fictitious capital can be both a source of wealth and a source of risk, as the value of these assets can fluctuate based on market conditions and investor sentiment.

INFORMATIONAL CAPITAL

Informational capital refers to the knowledge, skills, and technologies that are needed for the production and dissemination of goods and services. This type of capital is intangible but can have a significant impact on economic growth and innovation. It includes intellectual property, research and development capabilities, and access to information networks.

NATURAL CAPITAL

Natural capitals are the resources and ecosystems that provide essential services and benefits to human societies, water sources, fisheries, and biodiversity. These resources help in sustaining life and supporting economic activities, such as agriculture, tourism, and energy production. However, natural capital is often undervalued and exploited beyond its sustainable limits. That has, over the years, resulted in environmental degradation and loss of biodiversity.

IF THE SKY IS NOT THE LIMIT.

Most people have been brought up with limitations you get a salary with its limits / speed limits / time limits on products / working hours / contracts and lots of more these limits are all around us.

Now imagine a world without limits… is that even possible?

Yes, but you have to create it yourself.

Many people start their lives with high hopes. Some desire to make the most money among their age group, others want to end up being technocrats in their disciplines, who are forces to be reckoned with. All of these are achievable.

But the problem usually is most graduates eventually become employees of companies, where they always have to abide by rules and regulations set by someone else. Some of these rules may not be favourable to you as an employee. But who cares…. right. You just have to dance to the tune of the piper if you want to be paid.

Let's consider the limitations often encountered by people who work for others.

Lack of Autonomy: Working under someone else can sometimes feel like you're on a leash, constantly following orders and guidelines set by your supervisor or manager. This lack of autonomy can leave you feeling like you have little control over your own work. Research has shown that employees with limited autonomy tend to have lower job satisfaction and engagement levels, as they may not feel a sense of ownership or the freedom to explore new ideas in their role. It's important to recognize how this limitation can hinder your personal growth and development, as you may have fewer opportunities to take initiative or think outside the box.

Restricted Decision-Making Authority: When decisions are consistently made by someone else, it's easy to feel disempowered and frustrated. Not having a say in important matters that directly impact your work can lead to increased stress and dissatisfaction.

This lack of involvement in the decision-making process can also dampen your motivation and engagement. And guess what? It will eventually affect your productivity and performance.

Motivation and Engagement: Without the opportunity to contribute to decision-making, it's easy to feel less motivated and engaged in your work. The lack of autonomy in making decisions can leave you feeling disconnected and uninvolved in your role. This can hinder your ability to perform at your best and may lead to a decrease in overall job satisfaction and fulfilment.

Limited Creativity and Innovation: When you're constantly working under the direction and control of others, your creativity and innovation may be stifled. Without the freedom to explore new ideas and think outside the box, you might find yourself feeling uninspired and disconnected from your work. It can result in a lack of personal fulfillment and hinder your overall job satisfaction.

In a work environment that doesn't support creativity and innovation, you may struggle to feel engaged and motivated in your role. Research has shown that employees who feel their workplace is unsupportive of new ideas tend to have lower job satisfaction and higher turnover intentions.

To combat the limitations on creativity and innovation, you can advocate for a more supportive work environment that encourages new ideas and creative thinking.

Reduced Job Satisfaction: Sometimes, working under someone else can take a toll on your job satisfaction. Feeling like you have limited control over your work and decision-making can lead to decreased satisfaction levels. Studies have revealed that employees with less autonomy and decision-making authority report lower job satisfaction and higher stress levels. Also, the lack of opportunities for personal growth, creativity, and innovation can leave you feeling undervalued and unfulfilled in your role.

If you recognize the limitations of working under other people, such as the lack of autonomy, restricted decision-making authority, and others discussed in this section, it will help you manage your work environment more effectively and advocate for a more supportive and empowering workplace. And even more importantly, it will encourage you to own your own business and enjoy more freedom in your work environment.

DEFINE WEALTH.

Wealth has a different meaning for everybody a quiet life / a nice family / lots of money / a nice house / great food, whatever it is you like in life but that's not how professional financials define wealth.

Wealth is a multifaceted concept that can be viewed through different lenses, depending on one's background and expertise. While most of the population may perceive wealth as simply having enough money and possessions to live comfortably, a financial expert goes deeper into the intricacies of economic resources and liabilities.

A COMMON PERSPECTIVE ON WEALTH

When it comes to defining wealth, the majority of the population often simplifies it as having an abundance of money or material possessions. For many, wealth is synonymous with financial prosperity, the ability to indulge in luxuries, and the comfort of a secure lifestyle. It's about accumulating enough assets to afford the things that bring joy and fulfilment.

How the ordinary person on the street sees wealth or money:

DEFINING A GOOD LIFE

While money is recognized as a tool to pursue personal aspirations, some individuals find it challenging to pinpoint their true purpose in life. The concept of a “good life” may be elusive, leading to difficulties in aligning financial strategies with long-term goals. Clarity in vision and purpose is crucial for developing a sustainable financial plan that not only grows wealth but also nurtures personal fulfillment.

CLARITY AND PURPOSE

The non profession perspective on wealth acknowledges the role of money in achieving desires, but it also underscores the necessity of clarity and purpose. Without a clear vision of what constitutes a fulfilling life, financial strategies may lack direction and effectiveness.

PERSONAL GOALS

Wealth, from a not professional perspective, is a tool to fulfill dreams and aspirations. It serves as a means to achieve personal wishes and create a life of comfort and security. However, it is better to align financial strategies with individual goals and values. You should not only accumulate wealth but also cultivate a sense of purpose and fulfilment in your bid for wealth.

WHAT IS THE FINANCIAL EXPERT'S PERSPECTIVE ON WEALTH?

When it comes to defining wealth, a financial expert offers a more nuanced and comprehensive perspective. According to Investopedia, wealth is seen as the accumulation of valuable economic resources, encompassing both physical and intangible assets while considering debts. This definition provides a holistic understanding of an individual's financial standing, going beyond mere monetary value.

Financial experts take into account a broad range of assets, including physical possessions (like real estate and investments), as well as intangible resources such as intellectual property and trademarks.

In addition, financial experts also consider an individual's liabilities when defining wealth. They subtract debts from the total value of assets, to provide a more realistic assessment of one's financial situation. It ensures that individuals have a clear understanding of their overall financial standing and can make informed decisions to grow and preserve their wealth effectively.

Some of the items financial experts look at:

FOCUS ON MONETARY VALUE

The non expert perspective often centres around the idea of accumulating money and material possessions. It's a common belief that having a substantial amount of wealth equates to financial prosperity and the ability to afford luxuries. Money is perceived as a tool to achieve personal goals and desires, serving as a means to elevate one's lifestyle and secure a comfortable future.

For many individuals, the focus on monetary value is a driving force in their pursuit of wealth. The accumulation of money is seen as a tangible measure of success and security. Let's face it: it's not uncommon to associate wealth with the ability to purchase desired items, travel to exotic destinations, and enjoy life's comforts without financial constraints. Money becomes a desire to fulfill immediate needs and long-term aspirations.

This view of wealth is based solely on monetary value. It may overlook the broader spectrum of assets and resources that contribute to one's financial well-being. While money is undeniably important, a comprehensive understanding of wealth requires consideration of various economic factors beyond just the accumulation of cash.

Financial experts emphasize the need to diversify assets, manage liabilities effectively, and plan for long-term financial security to truly build and preserve wealth.

While money plays a significant role in achieving personal goals and securing a comfortable lifestyle, financial experts believe you to recognize the importance of a holistic approach to wealth management that considers a diverse range of assets, liabilities, and financial strategies.

HOLISTIC EVALUATION

Financial experts go beyond just looking at monetary assets. They consider a wider range of resources that contribute to an individual's overall wealth. This includes considering physical assets such as real estate, investments, and valuable possessions, as well as intangible assets like intellectual property and patents.

It also involves taking into consideration an individual's liabilities and debts. Financial experts understand the importance of subtracting liabilities from the total value of assets to get a clearer picture of an individual's financial health. This step ensures that the assessment of wealth is not skewed by financial obligations that need to be accounted for.

CLARITY AND PURPOSE

Without a clear vision of what you want to achieve with your wealth, it can be challenging to make informed financial decisions and prioritize your goals effectively. Here are some suggestions experts give on money-making:

Setting Clear Goals: Take the time to define what wealth means to you and what you want to accomplish with your financial resources. Whether it's saving for retirement, funding your children's education, or starting a business, having specific goals in mind can guide your financial strategies.

Aligning Your Finances: Once you have identified your financial goals, you should align your financial resources and strategies accordingly. It will involve budgeting, investing, and managing debt to ensure that your wealth works towards achieving your objectives effectively.

Seeking Professional Advice: Consider consulting with a financial advisor to help you develop a comprehensive financial plan that aligns with your goals and values. A professional can provide valuable insights and recommendations to optimize your wealth management strategies.

Revisiting and Adjusting: Periodically review your financial goals and strategies to ensure that they still are within alignment with your aspirations and circumstances. Life changes, economic conditions fluctuate, and priorities evolve, so it›s important to adapt your financial plan accordingly to stay on track toward building and preserving your wealth.

INTERGENERATIONAL WEALTH AND WHY IT IS IMPORTANT

Intergenerational wealth refers to financial assets passed by one generation of a family to another. Those assets can include cash, stocks, bonds, and other investments, as well as real estate and family-owned businesses. In last year's intergenerational wealth has become a focal point in discussions about the racial wealth gap and the increasing concentration of wealth in the world, because it plays a substantial role in both.

Intergenerational wealth transfer can be facilitated through various methods, including estate planning, trusts, Family office, wills, or gifting. By employing these strategies, families or family office can ensure that their wealth is preserved, protected, and distributed.

In ancient times, families had ingenious ways of passing down their wealth to ensure the prosperity of future generations. These strategies laid the foundation for long-term financial security.

Some different forms of wealth transfer can be:

Inheritance: Inheritance has long been a fundamental mechanism for transferring wealth from one generation to another. Ancient families valued the passing down of assets like land, property, and material possessions to their children upon their death, solidifying a legacy of prosperity. This practice preserved wealth and also instilled a sense of responsibility and stewardship in heirs.

Inheritance served as a means of providing security and stability for future generations. The transmission of wealth through inheritance was not merely about material possessions but also about preserving family values and traditions.

Through the act of inheritance, ancient families solidified their lineage and ensured the longevity of their wealth across generations. This time-honoured practice not only facilitated the transfer of assets but also symbolized a bond between past, present, and future family members.

Family Businesses: Family businesses provided a sustainable source of income and assets over generations.

These enterprises served as a vehicle for passing down valuable skills and knowledge from parents to their children, ensuring the continuity of wealth within the family lineage. Whether engaged in agriculture, trade, or craftsmanship, these businesses played a crucial role in building and preserving generational wealth. The hands-on experience gained through working in the family business contributed to financial success and fostered a strong sense of unity and purpose within the family.

In ancient societies, family businesses were more than just a means of financial gain – they were a symbol of tradition and heritage. The values instilled in the next generation through these businesses went beyond monetary wealth. They were used to emphasize the importance of hard work, dedication, and entrepreneurial spirit.

Education and Mentorship: Education to equip your children with the necessary skills and expertise to make informed financial decisions, and mentorship to provide a unique opportunity for them to learn from the wisdom and experiences of those who have successfully managed and grown the family wealth over time.

Trusts and/or Family office: These legal structures were established to manage and protect assets over time. They guaranteed a consistent source of financial support for descendants. Families could secure their wealth from external threats and fluctuations in the market, guaranteeing a stable foundation for generations to come through trusts or run it through a family office.

BASEL 1 -2 -3 CAPITAL REQUIREMENTS (IFRS) & (GAAP).

Basel (1-2-3) is a set of accounting rules for banks. **These rules do not apply for company's *but what if you test it on your company***, it can give you a deeper look into your financials and it can give you an extra auditable trace as well.

Basel rules are guidelines how much capital banks have to keep in their reserve based on the level of risk of their assets.

Basel I stands is the foundational framework for ensuring capital adequacy and risk management. Introduced in 1988, Basel I laid down the groundwork for minimum capital requirements that banks must maintain to cover potential losses. It requires banks to hold at least 8% of capital based on their risk-weighted assets. It aimed to promote stability in the banking sector and mitigate credit risk. This accord served as an important benchmark for financial institutions to assess and manage their capital reserves effectively. It set the stage for further developments in banking regulation.

As a company, the importance of maintaining a minimum amount of capital to absorb risks and ensure financial stability cannot be overstated. When you adopt a capital adequacy ratio based on risk-weighted assets, your company can enhance its resilience against economic uncertainties and unexpected events.

Basel I also underscored the significance of fair and standardized banking practices, emphasizing the need for transparent and reliable financial information to stakeholders. If you implement similar principles in your financial strategies, your company can strengthen its risk management practices and promote competitive equality in the industry.

Here are some key lessons that you can learn from Basel I and apply to your business strategy:

Importance of Capital Adequacy: Basel I underscored the necessity of maintaining a minimum amount of capital to absorb potential risks and ensure financial stability. Therefore, adhering to capital adequacy ratios based on risk-weighted assets will help your company fortify its ability to weather economic uncertainties and unexpected events.

Effective Capital Management: Basel I also highlighted the role of efficient capital management in mitigating risks and providing a solid financial foundation. This means that by adopting sound capital management practices inspired by Basel I can company optimize its resource allocation, enhance decision-making processes, and demonstrate financial robustness to stakeholders.

Promoting Fair and Standardized Practices: The Accord emphasized the significance of fair and standardized banking practices. It encouraged competitive equality among internationally active banks. Applying these principles to your company›s operations can enhance transparency, trust, and accountability within your financial framework.

Basel II refines risk measurement and management practices. This accord was introduced in 2004 and sought to enhance the alignment of capital requirements with the actual risks faced by banks. Basel II categorized assets into risk categories and utilized internal models for capital calculations. That provided a more sophisticated approach to assessing credit risk.

Lessons from Basel II for you to use in Your Company:

Adopt dynamic risk assessment models to accurately measure and manage risks. When you consider credit risk, operational risk, and market risk in your risk management framework, your company can make informed decisions and allocate capital more efficiently.

Your company should focus on comprehensive risk management that encompasses both quantitative risk measurement and qualitative risk management practices.

Basel II underscores the importance of balancing technical calculations with strategic risk mitigation strategies to enhance financial resilience.

The subprime mortgage crisis and the Great Recession of 2008 revealed the shortcomings of underestimating risks. That emphasizes the need for a holistic approach to risk management. Hence, companies need to heed the lessons from Basel II and ensure that their risk management practices are robust and adaptable to various scenarios.

Basel II also emphasizes the importance of understanding the risk profile of your assets and liabilities, enabling you to proactively identify and address potential vulnerabilities in your business operations. This enhanced risk assessment process can help you anticipate and respond to changing market conditions and regulatory requirements.

It encourages companies to implement robust quantitative risk measurement tools and qualitative risk management practices to enhance their risk governance. It combines quantitative data analysis with qualitative risk assessments, to help a company gain a comprehensive understanding of their risk exposure and develop tailored risk mitigation strategies. You are able to identify emerging risks, assess their potential impact on your business, and implement proactive measures to mitigate their effects.

Basel II's emphasis on risk governance underscores the importance of establishing clear roles and responsibilities within your organization to oversee and monitor risk management activities effectively.

Additionally, it highlights the significance of aligning capital requirements with the actual risks faced by your company. By maintaining a sufficient capital reserve based on the risk-weighted assets of your business, you can enhance your financial resilience and withstand unexpected economic challenges.

Basel III: In the wake of the global financial crisis of 2007-2009, Basel III sprung up to fortify the regulatory framework and bolster the resilience of the banking sector. This set of reforms introduced minimum capital requirements for market risk and emphasized the importance of liquidity coverage ratio and net stable funding ratio. It mandated additional buffers like the capital conservation buffer and countercyclical buffer. So, it sought to ensure that banks maintained adequate capital levels even during economic downturns. These measures were designed to enhance the stability and strength of financial institutions in the face of future crises.

Amidst the chaos of the financial crisis, Basel III underscored the critical need for effective risk management and robust governance practices within the banking sector. Companies can draw lessons from these principles and apply them to their own risk management frameworks.

They can prioritize liquidity and maintain sufficient capital reserves to enhance their ability to handle uncertain economic conditions and protect their financial stability.

The aftermath of the financial crisis served as a stark reminder of the importance of prudential regulation and risk mitigation strategies. Basel III's emphasis on maintaining adequate capital reserves and liquidity buffers resonates strongly with companies seeking to fortify their financial foundations. So, with the implementation of robust risk management practices and alignment with the principles of Basel III, businesses can enhance their resilience, and meet their obligations easily.

IMPLEMENTING (BASEL TYPE) REFORMS IN YOUR COMPANY

These are some key steps to consider when implementing Basel type principles in your company:

Assessing Capital Requirements: Evaluate your current capital reserves and ensure they meet the minimum requirements set forth by Basel III. Consider establishing additional buffers to withstand economic downturns and unforeseen events effectively.

Improving Risk Governance: Strengthen your risk governance framework by enhancing transparency, accountability, and oversight in your risk management processes. Promote a culture of risk awareness and compliance throughout your organization.

Enhancing Liquidity Management: Focus on maintaining adequate levels of liquid assets to address short-term funding disruptions and liquidity challenges. Implement robust liquidity risk management practices to safeguard your company›s financial well-being.

Adopting Proactive Risk Mitigation Strategies: Develop proactive risk mitigation strategies to identify, assess, and mitigate potential risks effectively. Monitor market developments, regulatory changes, and emerging risks to adapt your risk management approach accordingly.

IFRS REQUIREMENTS

In financial reporting, two major standards reign supreme: IFRS and GAAP. Understanding the key differences between these standards is crucial for companies seeking to present their financial information accurately and transparently.

While IFRS, issued by the IASB in London, promotes consistency and transparency on a global scale, GAAP is the go-to standard for public companies in the USA. The choice between IFRS and GAAP can significantly impact how a company reports its financial performance and position.

One notable contrast between IFRS and GAAP lies in revenue recognition. IFRS tends to be less rigid in defining revenue, allowing companies to recognize revenue sooner than under GAAP. This difference can lead to variations in reported revenue figures, influencing stakeholders' perceptions of a company's financial health. Understanding the nuances of revenue recognition under both standards is essential for accurate financial reporting and decision-making.

Another significant difference between IFRS and GAAP pertains to expense reporting. Under IFRS, expenses related to development or investments for the future may be capitalized instead of being immediately expensed. This divergence from GAAP reporting can impact a company's profit margins and overall financial outlook. Companies must navigate between these distinct requirements to present a true and fair view of their financial performance under either standard.

Managing the complexities of IFRS and GAAP reporting standards requires a deep understanding of the specific rules and guidelines outlined by each standard-setting body. While IFRS aims for global consistency and comparability, GAAP provides a structured framework tailored to the unique regulatory environment of the USA. Companies must carefully evaluate the implications of choosing between IFRS and GAAP. This is especially because they have to consider the impact on financial reporting practices and stakeholder perceptions.

When you clearly understand the foundation of capital adequacy in Basel I and the refinement of risk measurement in Basel II, you can improve your risk management practices and improve financial resilience. Applying the principles of Basel III post-financial crisis will further strengthen your company's ability to navigate complex banking regulations.

IFRS / GAAP summary:

- IFRS has been issued by the IASB International Accounting Standards Board who is based in London.
- IFRS was a replacement for the IAS system in 2001.
- IFRS is used all over the world, The USA does not use IFRS they use GAAP.

IFRS covers a wide range of accounting activities. There are certain aspects of the business practice for which IFRS sets mandatory rules.

Statement of Financial Position: This is the balance sheet. IFRS influences the ways in which the components of a balance sheet need to be reported.

Statement of Extensive Income: This can take the form of one statement or be separated into a profit and loss statement and a statement of other income, including Inventory, equipment or property and buildings.

Statement of Changes in Equity: Also known as a statement of retained earnings, these records show the company's change in earnings or profit for the given financial period.

Statement of Cash Flows: This report shows the company's financial transactions in the given period, separating cash flow into all operations, investing, and financing.

In addition to these standard reports, a company must give a summary of its accounting policies. The report is often seen as an appendix or side by side with the previous report to show the changes in profit and loss.

If there is a parent company involved it must create separate account reports for each of their subsidiary companies.

GAAP or Generally Accepted Accounting Principles, public companies in the USA are required to report with this system.

The differences between IFRS and GAAP reporting,

1. IFRS is not as strict in defining revenue and allows companies to report revenue sooner. A balance sheet using IFRS can show a higher stream of revenue than a GAAP version of the same balance sheet.
2. IFRS has different requirements for reporting expenses. If the company spends money on developing or investments for its future, it doesn't necessarily have to be reported as an expense. It can be capitalized instead.

Why is GAAP important? With a good set of accounting rules embedded in the structure of your organisation it can provide you with several benefits, and it will give banks and investors a reliable way to check and compare the financial results.

If you make these standards mandatory within your company, you can maintain a certain level of professionalism and at the same time your compliant with world standards.

The most important is the paper trail to follow for you to understand the financial lines within the company and for investors and banks to also see the financial structure and fundamentals.

NEW IFRS RULES IN THE FUTURE (IFRS 18 AND 19)

- In 2024, the International Accounting Standards Board (IASB) introduced two significant standards
- IFRS 18 (Presentation and Disclosure in Financial Statements) and
- IFRS 19 (Subsidiaries without Public Accountability Disclosures) which will be effective in 2027.
- It also is about to release narrow-scope amendments to IFRS 9 for power purchase agreements, which will be effective in 2026.

Its very important to keep up to date with these accounting rules even if you are not required to do so, you can take your lessons out of it to benefit and look at your own accounting systems.

THE BUILDING BLOCK SYSTEM.

What do i mean with a building block system?

Well, it is an ad on ad off system with various parts and components to build the solution to your challenges (or problems) and needs, or at least to get as close to the solution as is possible at that time.

When working toward the best solution possible at that time it can happen that the real solution will fall into your mind as you are progressing.

This is a simple to use system just start with establishing the end result (what do you want/need to achieve) and work from this as (BASE) and just take a few helpful tips or pieces of it and (glue or click) these together to form a new solution that fits your needs. (you can also work with post it memo's)

Now you not only have a Taylor made solution, but you own the system to create new ones as well.

You can use it over and over and with nearly everything in life.

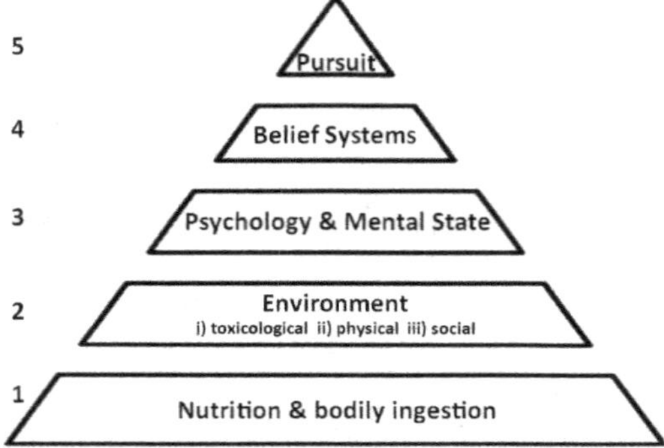

Just like this mental building block you can take solutions and ad on or off blocks to form the most idealistic situation to tackle your challenges. The solution building block works the same.

These building block systems are widely used in the industry and also in healthcare and mental care.

For a more detailed and academic approach to this topic you can look up “The Open Group Architecture Framework” (TOGAF)

TOGAF is the most used framework for Business architecture from 2020 off on, and it covers various disciplines within your company like, planning, governing, and much more.

BENEFITS OF USING THE BUILDING BLOCK SYSTEM

Better Communication: By breaking down complex concepts into smaller, more manageable building blocks, you can ensure that information is communicated effectively and efficiently. This approach promotes clarity and understanding among employees.

Promotes Streamlined Processes/Workflow Efficiency: With a structured framework in place, tasks can be completed more seamlessly, reducing the likelihood of errors and delays. This not only boosts productivity but also enhances the performance of your team because it helps them to focus on key priorities and deliver results in a timely manner.

Collaboration and Innovation: Since it gives a clear roadmap for communication and task delegation, teams can work together more cohesively to achieve common goals. Such a collaborative environment promotes creativity and idea-sharing. It will drive continuous improvement and growth for your organization.

ADAPTABILITY AND SCALABILITY

With a flexible framework in place, you can easily adjust and modify your processes to meet evolving needs and challenges. That makes your business to stay ahead of the curve and respond effectively to market trends.

ABOUT THE AUTHOR

My name is Martin van Helden (post
grad MBA) Author of amazing business
books and (Romantic) Thrillers.
My long history of owning several businesses,
Doing a lot of research and traveling all
over the world has given me the unique
Opportunity to write these amazing
educating and entertaining books.
Martin has a way writing to simplifying complex
material into an easy read and trough his deep passion
for businesses / accounting and all that has to do with

the finances of businesses and his (thriller) mysteries he writes with a certain depth in his storylines. He likes these books to be a base and encouragement for people to get the best out of life and their business. Martin likes people to use the solutions in the books as a "building block" type of system to form your own solution and optimizing the usage of these books.

CONCLUSION

Capital, in the context of business, refers to the financial resources that a company uses to fund its operations, its growth, and expansion. It is a key component of any successful business venture, and understanding how to manage and leverage capital effectively can mean the difference between growth (success) and failure.

One top secret to managing capital in business is diversification. This means spreading your investments across different industries, sectors, and asset classes to minimize risk and maximize returns (omni channelling). The strategy protects your business from the potential downfall of any single investment, while you still benefit from the growth of multiple ventures. Meanwhile, effective risk management is needed for business growth. It includes managing the risks associated with capital investments. Companies that succeed with capital often have robust risk management strategies in place, which include identifying potential risks, assessing their likelihood and impact, and implementing measures to mitigate or avoid them.

Good cash flow management is also an important aspect of capital management within your company. This involves monitoring and controlling the inflow and outflow of cash within your company to ensure that you always have enough liquidity to meet your financial obligations.

Smart investors try to maintain a healthy cash flow, to avoid the pitfalls of insolvency and bankruptcy.

We have also established that debt can be instrumental for financing business growth. But it must be managed carefully to avoid financial ruin. Companies that succeed with capital often have a well-defined debt management strategy in place as well, which includes identifying the most appropriate sources of debt financing, negotiating favourable terms, and maintaining a healthy debt-to-equity ratio.

While financial capital is essential for business success, companies that truly excel often invest heavily in their human capital. This means providing employees with the training, resources, and support they need to perform at their best, which can lead to increased productivity, innovation, and overall business success.

Another secret to capital management in business is the formation of strategic partnerships. Partnering with other companies or organizations often help businesses to pool their resources, share risks, and access new markets and opportunities that would otherwise be out of reach. This strategy helps them to leverage capital and achieve growth and success more easily.

One more very important thing in business is having multiple income streams (also known as omni- channelling) this secures your income and investment capacity, also if you have these omni-channels within other time zones around the world you will also benefit and make money while you sleep 24/7 and 265 days a year.

For complex financial advice make sure you get the right advisors on board even if you have to go to more than one, having the right advisor at the place can keep you from making costly mistakes or even get a lawsuit and these cost will always out way the cost of the mistake or reputation damage.

The secrets to capital management in business are not really secrets at all they are simply sound financial principles that, when applied consistently and thoughtfully, can lead to lasting success. They just don't occur as being important.

INDEX

The house of Medici: Malaguzzi, Silvia (2004). Botticelli. Ediz. Inglese. Giunti Editore. ISBN 9788809036772 – via Google Books.

The Medieval World – Europe 1100–1350 by Friedrich Heer, 1998 Germany

Amsterdamsche Wisselbank: Albert Scheffers (2020) Muntmeesterrekeningen bij de Amsterdamse Wisselbank

Phoonsen, Johannes (31 March 1677). "Berichten en vertoogen, raackende het bestier van den omslagh vande wisselbanck tot Amsterdam". by Jan Bouman – via Google Books.

Quinn, Stephen; Roberds, William (2023). How a Ledger Became a Central Bank: A Monetary History of the Bank of Amsterdam. Cambridge University Press. doi:10.1017/9781108594752. ISBN 978-1-108-59475-2. S2CID 265264153.

VOC First stock Exchange: Lodewijk Petram (2014) The worlds first stock exchange ISBN 9780231163781

University Amsterdam (2011) Lodewijk Petram.

University of Munich (2019) A Rjumohan paper nr:101855

Dubble - entry bookkeeping system: Lee, Geoffrey A. (1977). "The Coming of Age of Double Entry: The Giovanni Farolfi Ledger of 1299–1300". Accounting Historians Journal. 4 (2): 79–95. doi:10.2308/0148-4184.4.2.79. JSTOR 40697544. Archived from the original on 27 June 2017. Lee (1977), p. 80.

de Roover, Raymond (1963). The Rise and Decline of the Medici Bank, 1397-1494. Beard Books. p. 97. ISBN 9781893122321.

E3S web of Conferences 175, 13011 (2020) Interagromash 2020 "The definition of capital as an economic and accounting category"

Transition from barter to currency: Taskinsoy, J. (2018) Transition from Barter Trade to Impediments of the Dollar System: One Nation, One Currency, One Monopoly.. (Research Gate: SSRN Electronic Journal) DOI:10.2139/ssrn.3348119

Concept of the Invisible Hand: Bagha, Jacob and Laczniak, Gene R., "Seeking the Real Adam Smith and Miton Friedman" (2015).

Marketing Faculty Research and Publications. 208. https://epublications.marquette.edu/marketfac/208

Role of Central Banks in the Currency Market:

Board of Governors of the Federal Reserve System. “Reserve Requirements.” https://www.federalreserve.gov/monetarypolicy/reservereq.htm

Board of Governors of the Federal Reserve System. “Federal Reserve Actions to Support the Flow of Credit to Households and Businesses.” https://www.federalreserve.gov/newsevents/pressreleases/monetary20200315b.htm

Board of Governors of the Federal Reserve System. “The Discount Window and Discount Rate.” https://www.federalreserve.gov/monetarypolicy/discountrate.htm

Federal Reserve Bank of St. Louis. “Federal Funds Rate.” https://fred.stlouisfed.org/series/DFF

Bank of England. “What Is Quantitative Easing?” https://www.bankofengland.co.uk/monetary-policy/quantitative-easing

Great Depression of the 1930s: Romer, C.D, Pelks, R.H. (2024) Great Depression. (Britannica) https://www.britannica.com/event/Great-Depression

International Monetary Systems: Ocampo, J. (2016). A brief history of the international monetary system since Bretton Woods. (SSN 17987237 ISBN 9789292561413)

Cyber liability insurance: Agarwal, P. (. is cyber liability insurance an answer against growing cyber threats? Society for Underwriting Professionals.

- Abramovsky, A. and Kochenburger, P., 2016.

Insurance Onine: Reguation and Consumer Protection n a Cyber Word n the"

Dematerialsed" Insurance (pp 117142) Springer, Cham

- Biener, C., Eling, M. and Wirfs, J.H., 2018.

Harvard Business Review / The Importance of Organizational Design and Structure by Gill Corkindale February 11 2011

Insurablty of cyber risk. Methodoogy, p.9.

Chaisiri, S., Ko, R.K. and Niyato, D., 2015.

- August. A joint optimisaton approach to securityasaservice alocation and cyber insurance management In Trustcom/ BgDataSE/SPA, 2015 EEE (Vol. 1, pp. 426433). EEE.

New York Stock Exchange (NYSE): Why international companies choose NYSE, https://www.nyse.com/article/trading/d-order

Brauning, F. (2020). The Great Leverage 2.0? A tale of different indicators of corporate leverage. https://ideas.repec.org/p/fip/fedbcq/87795.html

Business Continuity Institute's Good Practice Guidelines: Business Continuity Institute. (2019). New Good Practice Guidelines (GPG) Edition 7.0 https://www.thebci.org/certification-training/good-practice-guidelines.html

Technology's (NIST) Framework for Improving Critical Infrastructure Cybersecurity: Barret, M.P. (2018). Framework for Improving Critical Infrastructure Cybersecurity Version 1.1. (National Institute of Standards and Technology) https://www.nist.gov/publications/framework-improving-critical-infrastructure-cybersecurity-version-11

Basel III: Laurens, F. (2012).Basel III and prudent risk management in banking: Continuing the cycle of fixing past crises. (Research Gate). DOI:10.22495/rgcv2i3art1

IFRS: Palmer, B. (2024). What Are International Financial Reporting Standards (IFRS). (Investopedia) https://www.investopedia.com/terms/i/ifrs.asp

HarvardBusinessReview/TheImportanceofOrganizational Design and Structure by Gill Corkindale February 11 2011

Graham Mcleod. A Business and Solution Building Block Approach to EA Project Planning. 6th The Practice of Entrprise Modeling (PoEM), Nov 2013, Riga, Latvia. pp.266-276, ff10.1007/978-3- 642-41641-5_19ff. ffhal-01474783f

Elena Kornyshova, Rébecca Deneckère. A Proposal of a Situational Approach for Enterprise Architecture Frameworks: Application to TOGAF. International Conference on Knowledge-Based and Intelligent Information & Engineering Systems (KES 2022), Sep 2022, Verona, Italy. pp.3499-3506, ff10.1016/j.procs.2022.09.408ff. ffhal-03686090

Jump up to:[a] [b] *Imai, Masaaki (1986). Kaizen: The Key to Japan›s Competitive Success. New York: Random House.*

Furterer, Sandra L.; Wood, Douglas C. (25 January 2021). The ASQ Certified Manager of Quality/Organizational Excellence Handbook. Quality Press. p. 344. ISBN 978-1-951058-07-4. Retrieved 18 June 2024.

"Net Asset Value". Corporate Finance Institute. Retrieved 2022-12-21.

Raymond James (August 9, 2011). "Glossary of Investment Terms". raymondjames.com.

AICPA Audit and Accounting Guide - Investment Companies May 1, 2007.

"A Guide To Understanding Mutual Funds" (PDF). Investment Company Institute.

MORE AMAZING BOOKS FROM THIS AUTHOR

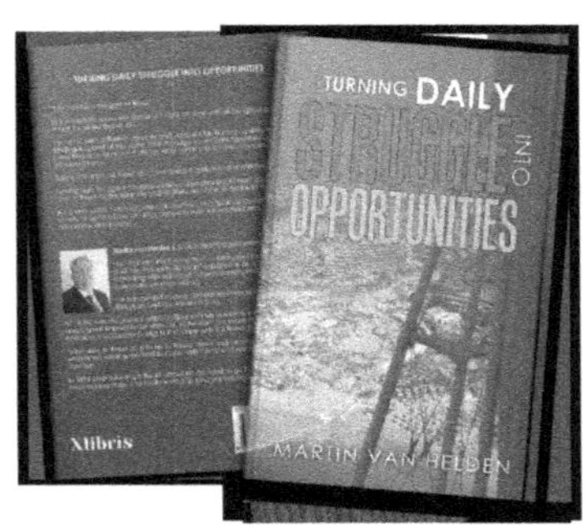

"TURNING DAILY STRUGGLE INTO OPPORTUNITIES" IS AN AMAZING SELF-HELP BOOK.

All Books are for sale at: AMAZON.com / E Bay.

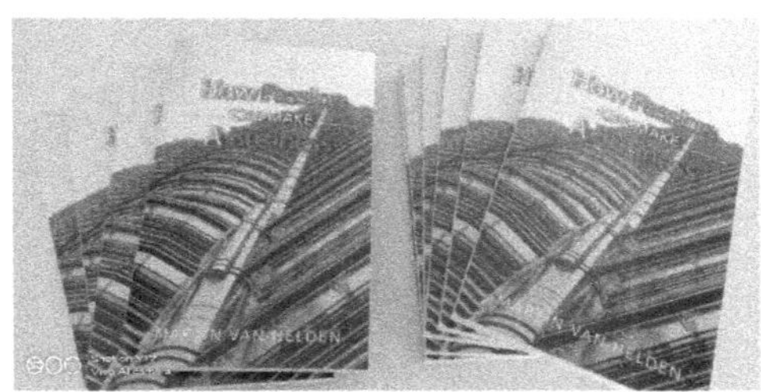

"HOW PASSION CAN MAKE A BUSINESS" IS AN EMPOWERING BOOK FOR ALL BUSINESS OWNERS.

www.Authormartin.com

www.ingramcontent.com/pod-product-compliance
Lightning Source LLC
Chambersburg PA
CBHW071330210326
41597CB00015B/1404

* 9 7 8 1 9 2 3 5 1 2 1 1 5 *